HOW TO COACH
FAST BREAK
BASKETBALL

HOW TO COACH

FAST BREAK

BASKETBALL

by Michael Esposito

• Englewood Cliffs, N. J. • PRENTICE-HALL, INC. •

Fourth printing .... *January, 1963*

TO MY WIFE,
Who Has Suffered Through Many
Games With Me

PREFACE

THE LAST DECADE HAS INTRODUCED A NEW STYLE OF ATTACK TO basketball—the fast break. Although every coach uses it at some time, not everyone fully understands the principles behind fast break basketball.

The purpose of this book is to set forth these principles. It is hoped that these fundamentals will aid high school and college coaches who wish to install the quick break in its entirety or wish to assimilate certain phases of it.

The book not only includes chapters on the development of this style of basketball, but also has chapters on how to play against it. Since every coach comes in contact with the fast break, either as part of his offense or to play against it, he should profit by reading the text.

TABLE OF CONTENTS

TERMINOLOGY

BASKETBALL HAS A LANGUAGE OF ITS OWN. ALL COACHES UNDER-stand the specific terms used. However, there are a few terms used in fast break basketball which need explaining. To facilitate reading the text, we shall explain below the meanings of the terms used throughout the book.

All-Court Press: A press applied by the defensive team whereby the opponents are picked up the moment they take the ball out-of-bounds.

Baseball Pass: A pass used in the fast break whereby the ball is thrown like a baseball with an overhand motion.

Bottle Zone: The zone formation often called 1-2-2.

Bounce Pass: A pass which is bounced from the passer to the receiver to penetrate a zone.

Break: A quick dart for the basket. Synonymous with Fast Break.

Chaser: In the 1-3-1 zone, the front man whose duty is to harass the outside men, forcing them to make bad passes or to take poor shots.

Combination defense: A defense combining the man-to-man with the zone.

Continuity: A play which is based on the same pattern but has different variations. The moment one variation fails the offense automatically moves into another.

Controlled break: An offense which fast breaks only on such occasions when an excellent opportunity to outnumber the defense exists.

Defensive Triangle: A situation where we have three rebounders around the basket, forming a triangle.

Deliberate Plays: An offense which carries out its play patterns in a slow, deliberate manner, so that each player carries out his assignment in a slower tempo than in the fast break.

Double Pivot: Two offensive men in the area near the foul line.

Double Team: Having two players cover one offensive man.

Drive In: To move at top speed toward the basket.

Driving Layup: An offensive player drives hard and fast to the basket and takes a shot, usually a layup, at close range.

Fast Break: The moment that a defensive team gains possession of the ball, either through a rebound, a score, or an interception, it makes a rapid movement toward the opponent's basket.

Floating: Playing a defensive player in such a way as to be able to cover another opponent as well.

Four on Three: An offensive situation wherein we find four offensive men covered by three defensive players.

Fundamentals: Those elementary basketball principles and skills necessary as a background for the more intricate patterns of the fast break.

Get the Inside: Playing between an opponent and the basket on rebounds or on defense.

Half-Court Press: Picking up opponents and pressing them the moment they step over the midcourt line.

Hook Pass: A pass that is thrown with a hooking motion of the arm to start the fast break.

Interception: When a defensive player steals the ball from an opponent by grabbing a pass intended for another opponent.

Layup Shot: A shot taken immediately under the basket.

Man-to-Man: A defense whereby each player of the defensive team plays a definite man on the opponent's team, attempting to keep his scoring down.

Middle Area: That part of the court straight down the center from defensive basket to offensive basket.

Middle Man: On the fast break, the offensive player going straight down the center of the court.

One-Three-One: A zone formation in which one man is up front, three men in the secondary line of defense, and one goal tender under the basket.

One-Two-Two: A zone formation in which one man is up front, followed by secondary and tertiary defensive lines of two men.

Pattern: Particular style of offense or defense that a team uses.

Pivot: An offensive man playing in the area near the foul line.

Playing Percentage: Playing that type of basketball where the odds are greater in your favor.

Post: An attack in which one player is in the pivot and the attack is directed toward him, with the hope of shaking a man loose.

Press: A defense whereby the player exerts such pressure, causing the offensive player to make mistakes or lose possession of the ball.

Quick Break: Same as fast break.

Scouting: Obtaining information about the opposition before the game.

Screen: A maneuver where a player is set up in a shooting position behind the camouflaging of another teammate who momentarily causes the guard of the prospective shooter to be blocked out of position.

Set Offense: An offense that uses a pre-arranged pattern of play.

Set Up: To prepare a defense or offense.

Single Pivot: One player in the foul line area.

Slough Off: Loosely covering a player or area in order to be in position to play another player or area.

Strategy: That command of basketball techniques which will enable one to outwit an opponent.

Switch: Two players changing opponents.

Switching Defense: Changing from a man-to-man to a zone or from one type of zone to another.

System: A team's basic set of offensive or defensive patterns.

Two-on-Two: A fast break situation that arises when three offensive men are covered by two defensive men.

Three-Two: A zone defense wherein we have three front men and two goal tenders.

Two-on-One: A fast break situation wherein the offense has the advantage of having two men covered by one defensive man.

Two-one-Two: A zone alignment wherein we find two men up front, one in the middle area, and two goal tenders.

Two-Three: A zone alignment wherein there are two front men and three goal tenders.

Zone: A type of defense wherein each defensive player covers a certain area of the court.

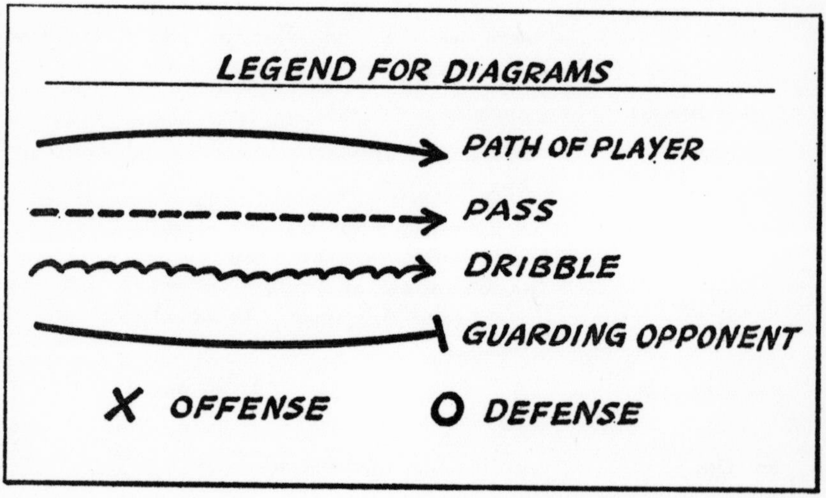

LEGEND FOR DIAGRAMS

⟶ PATH OF PLAYER

⤏ PASS

〰⟶ DRIBBLE

⟍ GUARDING OPPONENT

X OFFENSE   O DEFENSE

HOW TO COACH
FAST BREAK
BASKETBALL

1

PERFECTING THE BASIC
SKILLS FIRST

Before fast break basketball can be taught in high school
and college, the fundamentals of shooting, dribbling, passing, and
defensive work should be mastered. Without these fundamentals
the high school and college coach will have to spend much valuable
time in teaching them when he should devote himself to fast break
basketball.

SHOOTING

Since fast break teams depend greatly on shooting, much stress
should be placed on this fundamental. In junior high and high
school, boys should be taught the correct form in shooting and the
many varied shots now in use.

Two-handed shot. Teach the two-handed shot first. Since it is
the fundamental position from which passing, dribbling, and shooting originate, stress correct form and proper follow-through. The
point you, as coach, should emphasize is the position of the hands
after the ball is released.

One-handed shot. Since the one-handed shot has become so
prominent in modern basketball, the junior high and the high school
coach must devote some time to the techniques of this shot in order
to prepare the player for high school and college fast break basketball.

Proper co-ordination needed. Place great stress on the part
that the left hand plays in guiding the ball to the shooting hand, and on

1

the coordination required between shooting and jumping. If the jump is made before the ball is released, the shot will more than likely fail to hit its mark. The same holds true if the shot is made before the jump, for the player will be "putting" the ball instead of shooting it. Perfect synchronization is required. Anyone who has watched Paul Arizin, the great scorer of the Philadelphia Warriors, make this shot knows how important is the proper coordination between shooting and jumping.

The under-handed shot. The under-handed shot is taught because it is used to draw fouls in close guarding. Emphasize the correct form of releasing the ball under the hands of the guard. This is an important shot in the fast break, since many occasions arise when the driving player is confronted by a guard.

One-hand driving layup shot. The one-hand driving layup shot is the most important one in fast break basketball. Thus, it is the most fundamental part of shooting, since most of the scoring of breaking teams comes from this shot.

Have the player go off his left foot, if he is righthanded, and jump as high as he can, keeping his eyes on a spot six inches above the basket, where he is to place the ball. If you have your players follow this form constantly in practice, they will learn to make the shot automatically. This practice will simulate game conditions and will prepare for the many opportunities arising during the game.

DRIBBLING

The art of dribbling has become more and more important in modern-day basketball. In the fast break it is even more essential, because it is used to get into scoring position for quick layups. Anyone who has watched Bob Cousy of the Boston Celtics play knows that dribbling is of paramount importance in fast break basketball.

Most boys can dribble, but few can dribble well enough to elude their opponents. One need not be a Bob Cousy, but he should be skilled in dribbling past defensive players. He should have sufficient skill to drive into the forecourt for the all-important layup shot.

Drills help develop skill. Drills in which dribbling and shooting are combined are the best for developing skills. Drills which require players on the offense to keep the ball away from the defensive players by dribbling about the court help develop dribbling skills.

PASSING

Baseball and hook passes. The fast break depends on quick and accurate passing. Therefore, much stress should be placed on this fundamental. The two main passes required to initiate the fast break are the hook pass and the baseball pass.

After a rebound, the defensive player initiates the break by passing to a player cutting down the court. This pass is made in one of two ways. If he clears the boards without opposition, he uses a baseball pass. If he is guarded closely when he rebounds, he uses a hook pass, over the outstretched hands of the defensive player, to the player cutting down the court.

Loop, chest, and bounce passes. In addition to these two passes the player should know how to use the loop pass, the chest pass, and the bounce pass. Drills in which the loop pass is made by the guard to a cutting forward will help develop this type of pass. The loop pass is used to feed pivot men. The chest pass is used from guard to guard or guard to forward on deliberate plays. The bounce pass must be learned thoroughly, for it is used frequently against zone defenses.

DEFENSE

In modern-day basketball, defense is a lost art. Therefore, it is necessary that it be stressed more as a fundamental. There are three types of defense that the player must learn. These are man-to-man, zone, and press.

The man-to-man defense. The man-to-man defense is the most fundamental, since it makes definite assignments. This defense is difficult to learn because of the foot work required in close guarding. In this respect, the "shuffling" step is of primary importance. Distance is important also. If the defensive player is too close, he invites the opposing player to dribble around him. On the other hand, if he stays too far, he invites set shots over his head. Drills in which both faults are exaggerated will tend to teach the defensive player the correct distance.

Zone defense. The zone defense, which is the most frequently used for fast breaking, requires the player to move about in such a way as to prevent too many set shots to be taken. The zone must be played in such a way as to harry the offense sufficiently to force it to hurry its shots. Many rebound opportunities result from this type of defense. For this reason the zone defense is an effective one for breaking.

The 2-3, 2-1-2, 1-3-1, and 1-2-2 zones. Since there are many zone defenses, the player must learn the strength and weakness of each one. The 2–3 zone is strong for rebounding but weak against set shooting. Therefore, a fast break team which plays against a weak outside shooting team should use this particular defense. The 2–1–2 is strong around the basket but weak at the sides. The 1–3–1 protects the sides but is weak at the corners. The 1–2–2, or bottle zone, is weak at the corners, but it is strong for breaking.

Press defense. The press defense is used more and more today. A good fast break team should master the press to use against poor ball handlers. The press defense is used in the closing minutes of the game when a team is behind, as well as during the game to keep the opposing team off balance.

The fast break team must be instructed in all phases of these defenses because each one is used at various stages of the game or at sometime during the season.

During the formative years in the junior high or in the high school, the player who learns these fundamentals is preparing for fast break basketball.

Drill for fast break. Coaches should drill for the quick break by having players move down the court rapidly, attempting to use these fundamentals while moving at top speed. Undoubtedly the player will make many mistakes, but he will be preparing himself for the fast break.

Learn skills before fast breaking. The college coach will find that his players are not ready to learn fast break fundamentals if they are not well schooled in these preliminary skills. If he finds that his freshmen are lacking in these skills, it is better that he has them learn these skills during this first year before he attempts to teach them fast break basketball.

2

SELECTING PERSONNEL FOR THE FAST BREAK

Selecting the personnel for the fast break is far more involved than it is for the more deliberate style. Since the success or failure of a team is dependent upon its personnel, you must use great discretion in choosing. Each player you select must fit into your pattern. One poor selection can wreck the entire team.

Ideal forwards are fast and graceful. The players who develop best as fast break forwards are gazelle-like individuals who can move with speed and grace. Tall, thin boys best fit this requirement. In high school a height of 6′ to 6′3″ is ideal; in college, from 6′3″ to 6′6″ is necessary. Height in itself would not suffice if it were not accompanied by grace of movement. This is necessary to enable the player to move with effortless speed down court, to fake his opponent out of position, and to be able to feint and pivot before driving.

Forward must master at least one shot. The forward must have mastered at least one shot to perfection. Although it is desirable to have the player use hook shot, jump shot, two-handed set shot, underhanded shot, and drive-in layup shot when the occasion arises, he must become a specialist in one of these to be able to score freely.

Defensive skill is necessary also. Defensively he should be able to guard a man well enough to keep him from driving in at will or set shooting over his head. Too many players feel that if they score well on the offense that they need not worry about defense. This is a fallacy in strategy because common sense tells us that a player scoring twenty points per game and allowing twenty five

5

against him is not much use to his team. A boy scoring five points and allowing three per game is far more valuable.

The importance of defense is best exemplified by the Boston Celtics. Until they acquired Bill Russell, the defensive specialist, they were being outscored by other teams, despite the fact that they were the highest scoring team in professional basketball history. Their star players would score twenty five points per game and yet be outscored by their opponents. This defensive weakness kept them from winning the professional title.

Fast break guards are different from guards in other styles. In developing high scoring guards, always impress them with the fact that they must guard well also. The guards in fast break basketball are quite different from guards in other styles. In the more deliberate style the guard is usually the smaller member of the team, although quite agile. He shoots well from the outside, sets up plays, and acts as floor general.

The guard must be tall and rugged. In fast break basketball such a player would be out of place. The fast break guard must be tall, rugged, and a good rebounder. He must be able to start the fast break with his rebounding. He must get that initial pass out to the cutting forwards. It would be desirable to have him set shoot well, but that skill is not all-important. Nor is it necessary for him to drive in well, for, lacking these abilities, he will be stationed inside where his bulk and rebounding are advantageous under the basket. The forwards would then take the places outside where the guards usually play.

The guard plays inside on offense and defense. In this set up the function of the guard is to help offensively and defensively under the baskets. Thus, it is quite essential that he be rugged; he must love to "scrap" for rebounds. In the zone defense, which most fast break teams use, his place is under the boards, along with the center. If a 2–3 zone is used, the guards flank the center on either side. If a 2–1–2 zone is used, more than likely he will occupy one post under the basket with the center holding the other position, or the guards may occupy both positions under the basket with the center in the middle. In the 1–3–1 zone, he occupies one of the three lanes near the basket, with the center playing the position directly under the basket. In man-to-man defenses, he plays inside, guarding the corner.

The center must be versatile. The center in the fast break is a more versatile player than he is in other styles. He must rebound well on the offense as well as on the defense. On offensive plays he must often lead the break down court. Defensively, the center is often stationed near the basket to capture rebounds and set off the break. If the team plays a man-to-man defense, he plays the opposing pivot man and is in the best position to rebound.

The center must avoid swarming tactics of opponents. He makes the initial pass for the break when he captures the rebound. It may be necessary for him to dribble away from the opposing pivot man and thus avoid being tied up. Most teams will attempt to prevent the initial pass out and thus stop the break. The center must be aware of this strategy and counteract swarming tactics.

Center plays near the basket in various zones. If the zone is used, the center will receive more help from the guards, who should help him gain control of the boards. In the 2–3 zone, he usually occupies the middle position of the defensive triangle, unless one of the guards is a better rebound man. In such a case, the center would play either the right guard or left guard position in the 2–3, while one of the guards would take his place in the middle. In the 2–1–2 zone, he plays as one of the back men or in the middle of the triangle. In the 1–3–1 zone, he plays the back position under the basket.

Center plays the pivot and leads the fast break. Offensively he should be a tower of strength when the break stalls. On more deliberate plays, he is in the pivot. Offensive rebounding should be his forte. On breaking plays he should lead the break down court. He occupies the middle lane and follows up all shots taken. When the forwards shoot, he moves in for rebounds and tap-ins. Whenever the middle lane is open, he drives in for shots. Despite his size, he should dribble well.

Time reaction of personnel. In addition to personal observation, there are certain drills that can help in selecting personnel. One of the best of these drills tests reaction time of players. At a given signal players will run to certain designated spots. Time the reaction of each player.

A variation of this drill will have players run to spots where you throw the ball. In this drill you not only test the reaction time of the players but also their observational powers and powers of anticipation.

Test rebounding skill of guards and centers. There are several drills that test guards and centers. In one, you place a guard on each side of the basket and an opponent on the side of the guard. Then shoot at the basket, instructing the guard to capture the rebound from his opponent. Alternate shooting from opposite sides to give both guards a chance at the rebounds. Observe how high the guard jumps, how he uses his body to screen off his opponent, and how well he rebounds. This test is used for centers as well as for guards, since it tests rebounding ability.

3

PRE-SEASON TRAINING FOR FAST BREAKING

Training for the fast break is quite different from training for other styles of basketball since the player must attain far better physical condition. Since the fast break player must have great stamina to outlast his opponent, he must reach a physical condition which will enable him to run at top speed for long periods of time. In athletics the saying is that the legs are an athlete's chief asset. The fastbreak player is lost without legs that can endure the most gruelling test. Hence, you must work towards gaining this peak condition.

Program is set up. Physical conditioning must begin very early in the school year. Gather your players in September, or not later than October. At this time outline a program of conditioning which the players follow daily on their own. Though you may not have group practice more than once a week during this early training period, check carefully to see that your players carry out the program.

Calisthenics for leg development are selected. The early period of conditioning should begin with calisthenics. Since the chief aim is to develop strong legs, select calisthenics that will help gain this goal. Knee bending and leg stretching exercises which limber leg muscles are excellent at this early stage. There are many such exercises and drills used by football teams that could be adopted by fast break teams. These exercises and drills should continue until the more serious running program begins.

Two week program of running undertaken. After a few weeks of this preliminary program, the basketball season's training

9

ɔd gets seriously underway. For a period of two weeks, stress
⸺ drills intended to develop stamina or "wind." This last phase
of pre-season conditioning is devoted to running, preferably out-
doors. Beginning with one lap around the track, the player increases
his distance until he is running eight laps daily.

Gruelling test begins the second week. The second week the
more gruelling phase begins:

> *First day* ....player trots one lap, runs another at top speed.
>
> *Second day* ......player trots one lap, runs one, trots another,
> runs another.
>
> *Third day* ....player trots one lap, runs one, repeating the
> cycle three times.
>
> *Fourth day* ......player alternates the trot-run cycle four times.

The rest of the week he follows the running program of the fourth
day. This test develops stamina as well as strong legs.

Players should be encouraged to run cross country. If at
all possible, your players should be encouraged to run cross country,
not so much for achievement as for conditioning. The player who
undergoes this rigorous running routine will be able to play the
entire season at top speed, without ever worrying about tiring. Only
then can he truthfully say he is ready for the fast break.

***Basketball drills help condition players while developing
fundamentals.*** The last phase of the conditioning period should be
devoted to basketball drills which help develop fundamentals while
keeping legs limber. The following are sugggested drills for this
phase:

- Player dribbling at top speed down court.
- Two players passing to each other while moving the ball down
  court.
- Three men weaving from one end of the court to the other.
- Two men using the press against two offensive men.
- Three men fast breaking after a rebound.
- Four men fast breaking after a rebound.
- Two men on defense against three offensive men.
- Three men on defense against three offensive men.

- Five men weave from one end of the court to the other.
- Five men fast breaking down court.

These drills not only develop leg power but also give adequate training in the fundamentals of passing, dribbling, and defensive play. They also give an insight to the specific talents of the different members of the squad.

4

GRASPING
FAST BREAK FUNDAMENTALS

THE LAYUP SHOT IS THE MOST FUNDAMENTAL OF ALL FAST BREAK requirements, since it accounts for most of the scoring. The shot must be taught so that it becomes automatic. In order to assure a minimum of misses, certain drills are set up that teach precision.

THE LAYUP SHOT

Form two lines on opposite sides of the basket, with each line alternating in shooting. Teach the players to drive in fast for the layup shot. Then have them practice the layup shot without being harassed. After they have learned to make the shot with a fair amount of success, place players on the opposite line, instructing them to prevent the layup shot, thus simulating game conditions. When a player learns to shoot well under pressure, he is ready for whatever opposition may arise in games.

Early in the season as much as thirty minutes of daily practice is necessary. When precision is acquired, it can be cut down considerably. You may find that players become bored with this daily routine and may become sloppy in their shooting. To offset this, keep the drills interesting. As soon as you see boredom setting in, resort to some of these tactics to create interest.

1. Have the players count the number of layup shots made consecutively. Record the number and have players aim at breaking this record at each practice. This drill tends to keep players on their mettle in shooting.

12

No. 1: As the offense shoots, the defense takes good block-out positions. The idea is to stick with the offensive men, keeping between them and the basket, until direction of rebound is determined.

—All photographs courtesy of Scholastic Coach Magazine.

No. 2: Inside man has recovered rebound, turned, and is ready to pass out to side man. Middle man is moving into position for pass from side man and other front man is moving to fill the third lane.

No. 3: The middle man has received the pass from the side man and is turning up the court. The second deep man (who did not recover the rebound) is starting to take the essential trailer position.

No. 4: The ball has moved from the middle man to the side man and is now being returned to the middle man as a three-on-two situation develops. The three offensive men keep spread as they come down.

No. 5: Middle man has drawn defense out of position with a nice body fake to his left and slips a bounce pass to the teammate on his right. A smart defensive man would never have advanced so far up.

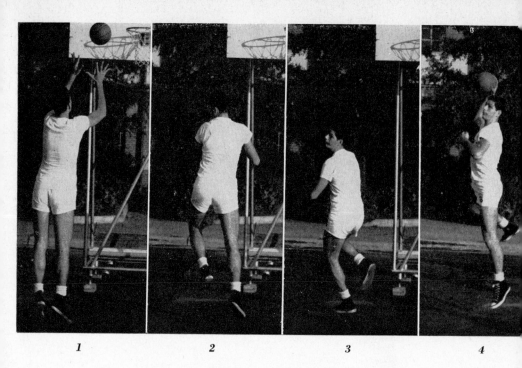

1   2   3   4

No. 1: Ball comes off rim following shot by opponent. No. 2: Guard takes ball. No. 3: Guard turns, looks for receiver. No. 4: Guard makes the pass out using a baseball pass.

Photographs courtesy of Athletic Journal

5   6

No. 5: The right forward receives the pitch out. No. 6: The right forward passes to the man in the middle lane.

8

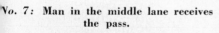

No. 7: Man in the middle lane receives the pass.

No. 8: Man in the middle lane dribbles down the center area.

No. 9: Man in the middle lane passes to his left forward under the basket.

9

2. Reward winners of drills. Eliminate those players who miss
    until only one remains, and then excuse the winner from
    practice early. Under such conditions players learn to con-
    centrate so much on accuracy that they will make more than
    100 layups without a miss.

Three points of layup shot. Three factors must be stressed in
making the layup shot properly.

1. The player must be sure to go off his left foot if he is right
    handed, or off the right foot if he is left handed.
2. He must be some three feet away from the basket as he goes
    up for the shot.
3. He must focus his eyes on a spot six inches over the rim
    and to the right of it.

The shot should be made softly with the fingers. Players who
use their palm in laying up the shot or who shoot too far away from
the basket lose accuracy. Another fault, causing inaccuracy, is for
the player to fail to look up at the spot over the basket. Some players depend on finger control to make the shot, but this is not as accurate as the method outlined above.

PASS OUT

Another important fast break fundamental is the pass out. Without the initial pass, there is no fast break. One of the best drills
to develop accurate pass outs is the one shown in Diagram 1.

Drills for guards help develop rebounding. Shoot at the
basket. The guard rebounds and hits one of three players who break
down court as soon as the ball is shot.

After guards have become accurate in this routine, make it tough
for them by having a player try to prevent them from rebounding.

If the guard gets tied up, he dribbles off to the right or the left to
clear himself and then passes out. The pass he uses depends on the
situation. If he is clear, the baseball pass is best. If he is covered,
a hook pass has a better chance to clear the outstretched hands of
the opponent.

DRIBBLING

Dribbling plays an important part in setting up scores in the fast
break. To develop fast dribbling, place forwards at the right and

the left side of the court, with the center in the middle. The two guards are on the defense. The center passes off to either side; the forward then dribbles as rapidly as he can down court. When the guard moves over to cover him, he passes to the center. The latter in turn dribbles as fast as he can down court. When the guard covers him, he passes to the other forward who dribbles in for the shot. See Diagram 2.

Daily practice of this drill will develop dribbling under game conditions and will carry over to games.

SHOOTING

Accurate shooting is the last fundamental of fast break basketball which requires emphasis. The following drill will help develop accurate shooting:

- Station two forwards at the side of the court and a center at the middle.

- Have two defensive guards cover the three men.

- The three men begin to pass to each other.

- The two defensive guards move over rapidly to cover the receiver of the pass.

- The moment that one of the three is uncovered, he shoots.

This drill tends to help develop accurate shooting under stress conditions.

TWO-ON-ONE FAST BREAK

To develop fast break thinking certain patterns should be practiced daily. Players must recognize immediately when they see a break situation. These opportunities occur whenever the defense is caught with one or two fewer men in position than the offense. When such occasions arise, the fast break offense immediately goes into its three lane drive.

Daily practice of these various drills will make breaking automatic. Two-on-one situations arise in the forecourt when interceptions occur. As soon as the interception occurs, the players go into action. See Diagram 3.

O^1 passes to O^2 but X^2 intercepts. As soon as X^1 sees this, he breaks away from O^1. X^2 dribbles down court fast. If O^1 comes over to cover him, X^2 passes to X^1. If O^1 covers X^1, X^2 dribbles in

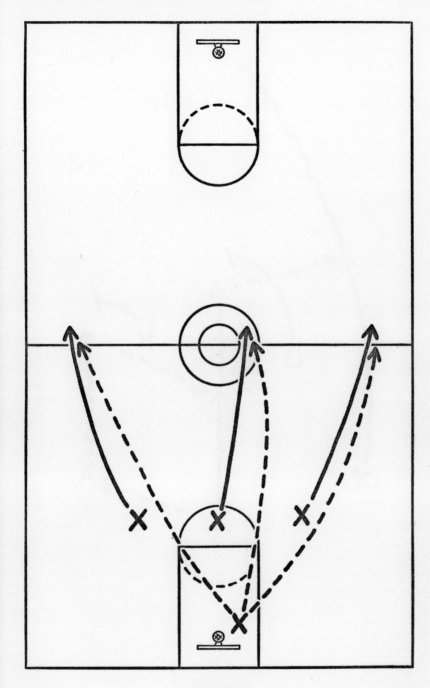

Diagram 1.

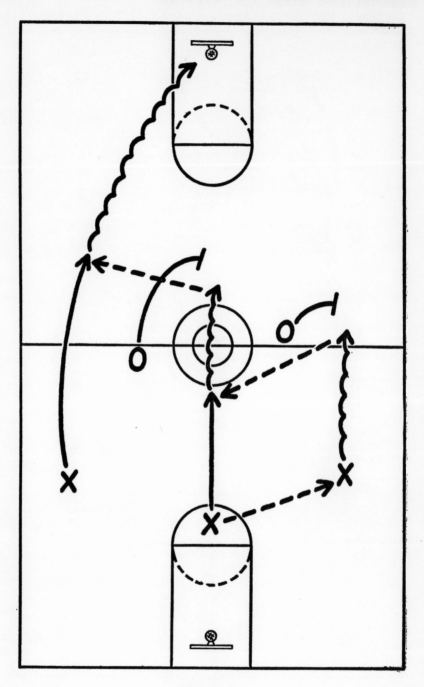

Diagram 2.

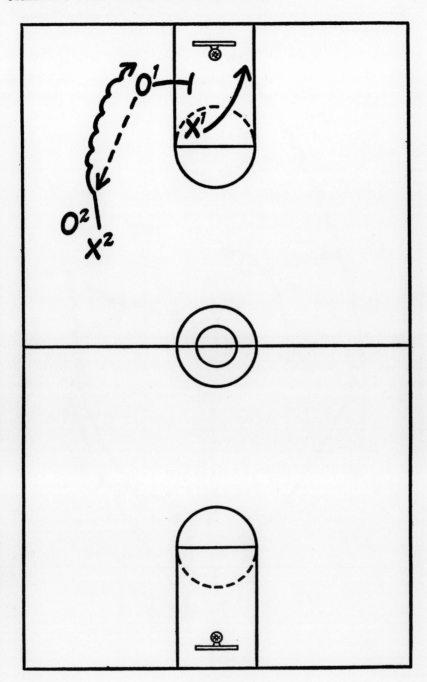

Diagram 3.

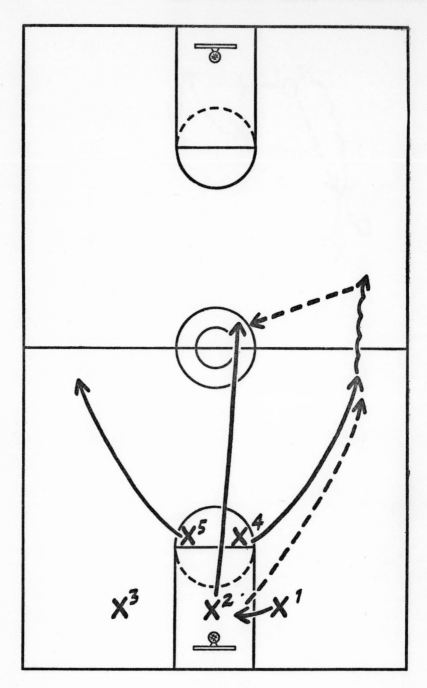

Diagram 4.

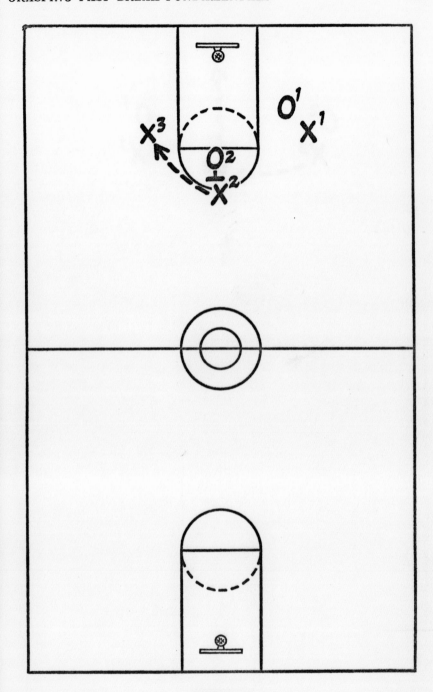

Diagram 5.

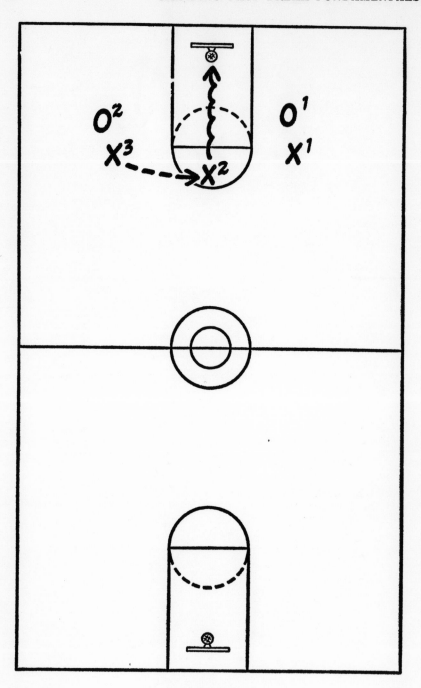

Diagram 6.

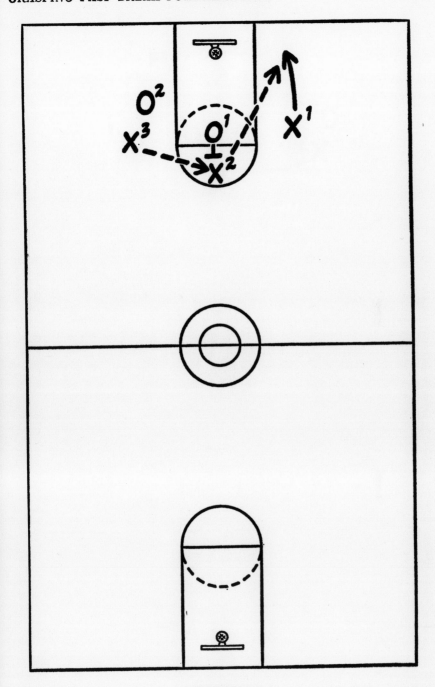

Diagram 7.

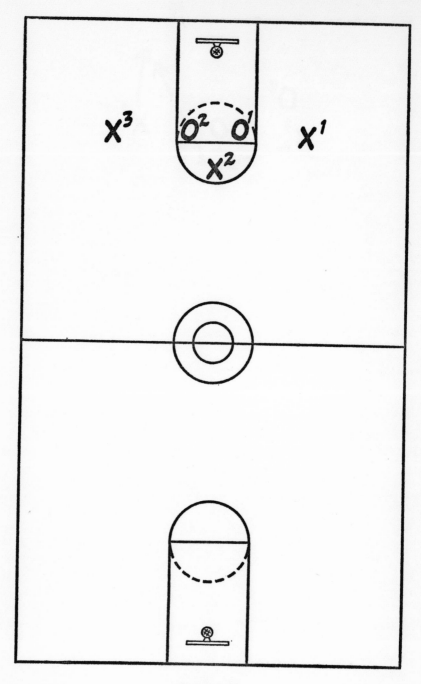

Diagram 8.

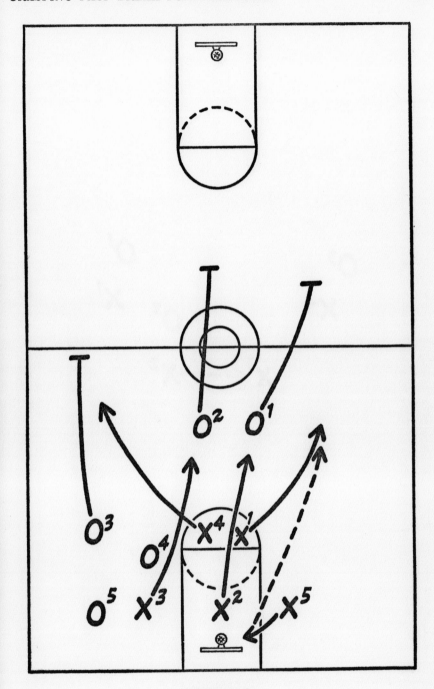

Diagram 9.

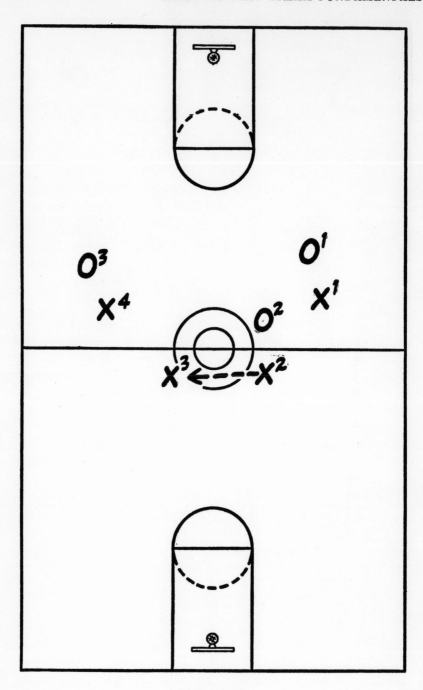

Diagram 10.

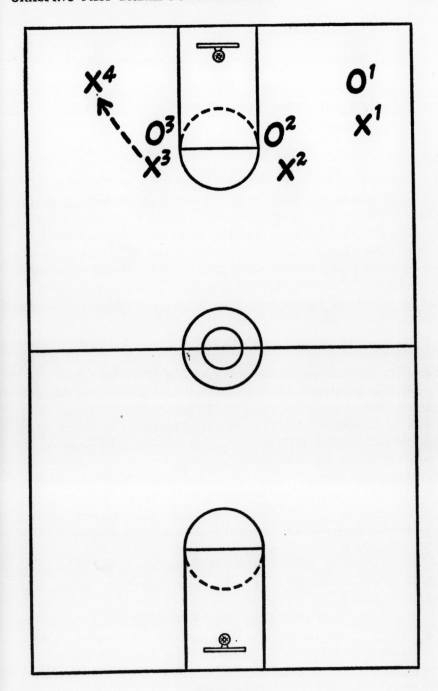

Diagram 11.

for the shot. If O^1 plays it smart by remaining between the two, X^2 keeps dribbling in to the basket. If O^1 does not make an effort to stop him, he shoots. The moment that O^1 commits himself, X^2 will pass to X^1.

These situations may not occur more than three or four times in a game, but if the offensive club can capitalize on them, it may win close games.

THREE-ON-TWO FAST BREAK

A good breaking team will get a three-on-two during the game on many occasions. If it can control the defensive boards, there may be some thirty or more such situations. If fifteen of these opportunities lead to baskets, the team will be in enviable position offensively. Since these opportunities occur so frequently, drills that teach how to manipulate the ball for quick layups are invaluable to the offensive team. A drill that teaches this is given in Diagram 4.

Guard starts fast break. Place two guards on the defense and two offensive men up front, where they would be to guard their opponents. Shoot from the side. As soon as one of the three defensive men gets the rebound, he throws to the right side. One of the two men who does not get the rebound goes down the middle lane.

Middle man controls break. The player on the right side dribbles as far as he can, drawing in his guard. Then he throws to the man in the middle lane. The latter dribbles as far as he can. If the guard on the other side comes over to play him, he passes to the forward on the left side. See Diagram 5.

If the two players retreat into the forecourt and the player in the middle lane passes to the left side, the latter dribbles in until his progress is impeded by one of the defensive players. He then passes to the player in the middle lane who dribbles in for the shot. See Diagram 6.

If the guard on the right side covers the center, the latter passes to the player on the right side. The latter dribbles in for the shot. See Diagram 7.

A difficulty may arise if the two defensive players keep drifting into the forecourt, covering the three men. The three offensive players must then dribble and manipulate the ball in such a fashion as to draw one of the guards out of position. If they fail to do so, the man in the middle lane shoots and drives in hard for the rebound. He must play some six feet behind the two forwards on the sides, so that he cannot be covered too well by the defensive men. See Diagram 8.

Daily practice of this drill will make three lane breaking automatic.

FOUR-ON-THREE FAST BREAK

Good defensive clubs often set up their defense in such a way as to cover the three areas. When this happens, a good breaking club must be prepared to have four men on three. If four lanes can be covered offensively on the break, the three men will be spread out too much to cover the extra man effectively. The drill shown in Diagram 9 will help develop a good four on three break.

As soon as the right guard obtains the ball, he hits the right forward. The latter will be covered by one of the two guards, so he passes to the center lane. He dribbles but is soon covered by the other guard. He then passes to the offensive guard X^3, who has come down court parallel to X^2. See Diagram 10.

This guard dribbles fast down court. If O^2 comes over to cover him, he passes back to X^2 who goes in for the shot. If O^3 covers him, he passes to X^4. See Diagram 11.

5

RECOGNIZING
FAST BREAK OPPORTUNITIES

Many opportunities arise during a game when you can take advantage of fast break situations. The most common occurrences take place after your opponent has missed a foul, after the tap, after a held ball, after a rebound, or after a score.

AFTER A FOUL

When your opponent misses a foul and you capture a rebound, certain pre-arranged alignments will make it possible for you to fast break. See Diagram 12.

O^3 misses a foul and X^1 captures the rebound. He tosses to X^4 who dribbles, drawing O^4 over to cover him. He then passes to X^3 in the middle lane. X^3 dribbles until O^5 comes over to cover him. Then X^3 passes to X^5 who drives in for the shot.

The key player in this break is X^3. He should drive down court fast before O^3 recovers to go on the defense. Since O^3 has his back to the opponent's basket and since he is concentrating on making his foul, he is often unprepared to get back on defense.

If O^3 makes this break difficult by dropping back on defense, X^2 can break into the center lane in his place. If X^3 and X^2 both break, they will make it difficult for O^3 to cover both. See Diagram 13.

AFTER A TAP

At the center jump beginning each period, it is possible for you to fast break if you get the tap. Diagram 14 illustrates the alignment and pattern of break.

28

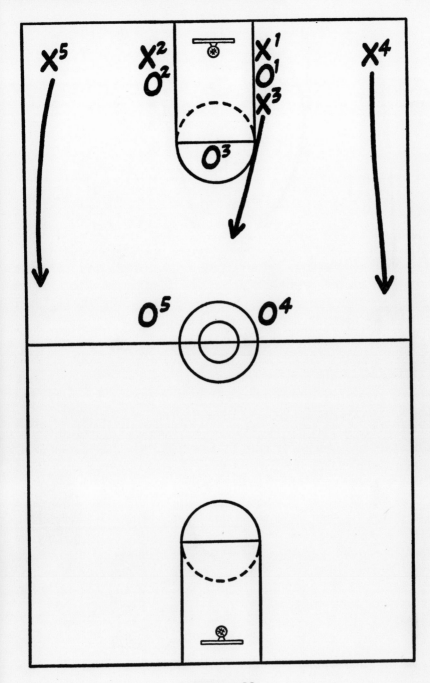

Diagram 12.

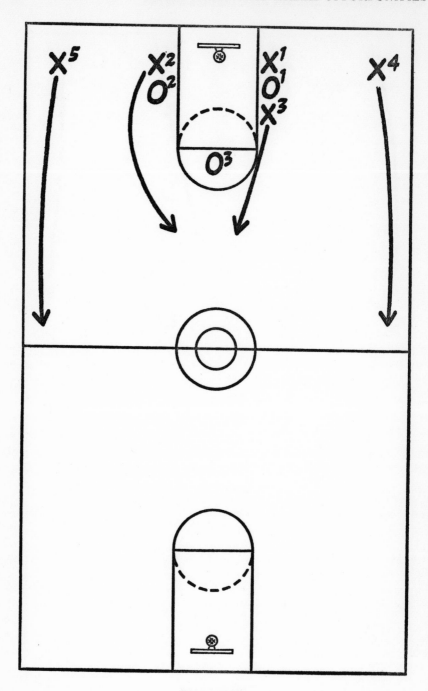

Diagram 13.

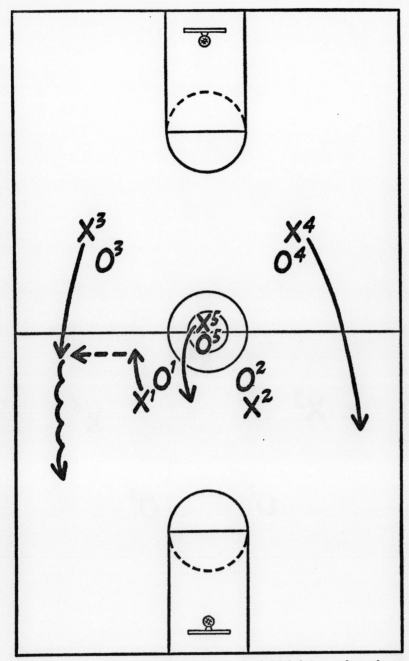

Diagram 14. The writer has his forwards play behind their guards on the tap because from his experience he has found it is easier to control the tap in this formation than in the orthodox lineup.

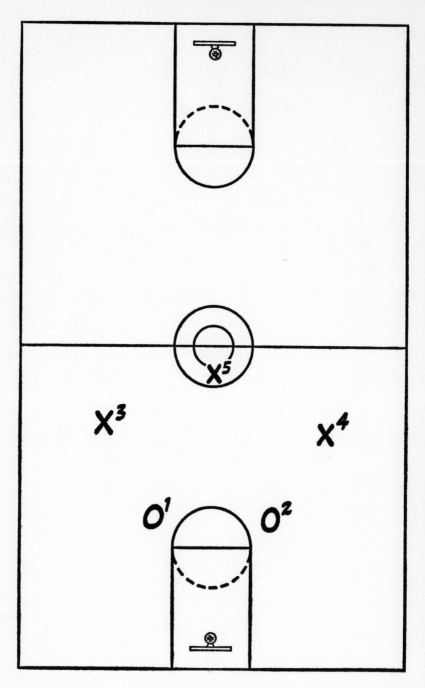

Diagram 15.

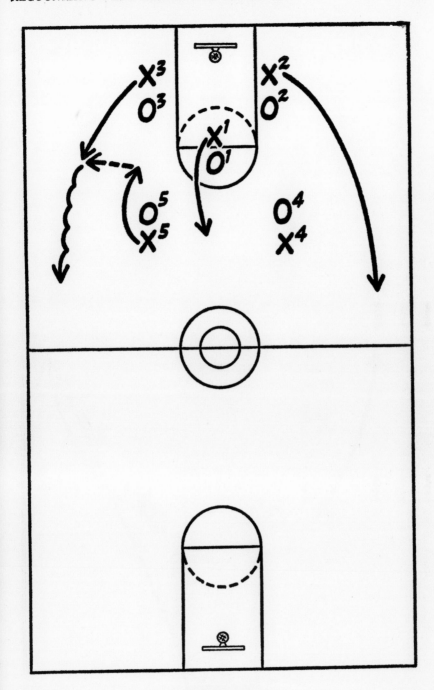

Diagram 16.

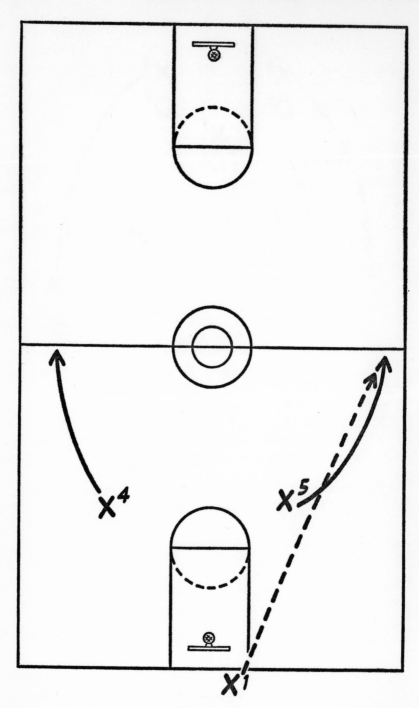

Diagram 17.

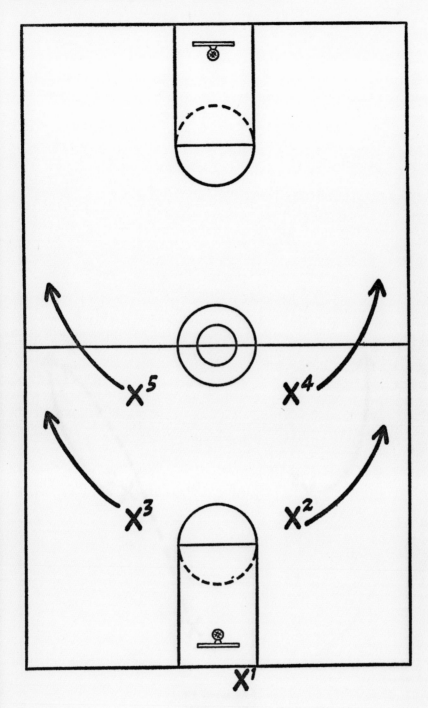

Diagram 18.

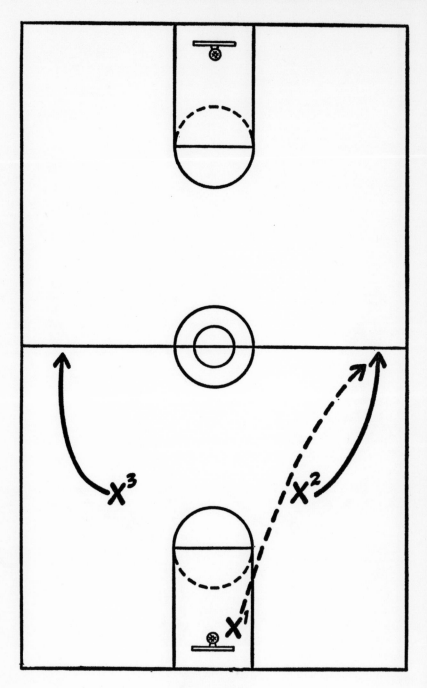

Diagram 19.

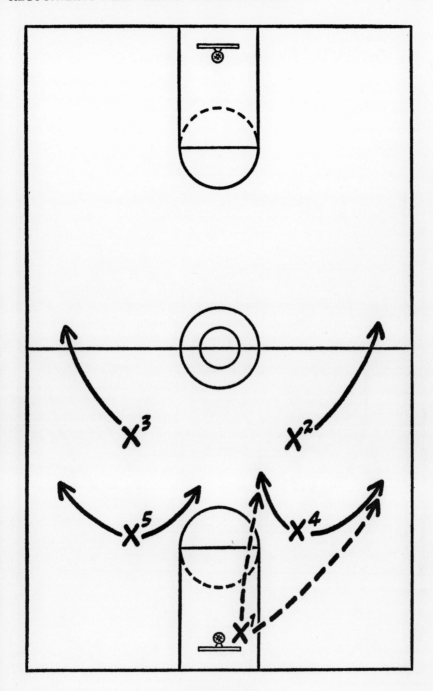

Diagram 20.

Let is say X^5 gets the jump. On the tap X^5 hits the ball to X^1, who comes around O^1. X^1 immediately passes to X^3 who drives down the right side. X^4 meanwhile has come down the left side. X^5, after the tap, has come down the center lane, so that the three men will have the positions shown in Diagram 15.

It is an easy matter for X^3 to drive in, bringing O^1 to cover him. X^3 then passes to X^5 who drives in unmolested or passes off to X^4 for the shot.

AFTER A HELD BALL

A held ball is much like the opening tap-off since the relative positions of the players are the same. If the held ball is near your defensive basket, then the break is possible. Diagram 16 shows how this takes place.

X^1 taps to X^5 who passes to X^3. The latter dribbles down court. Meanwhile X^2 goes down the sideline and X^1 comes down the center lane. From there on the offensive maneuvers are the same as in the center jump, since you will have three offensive players on two defensive players.

AFTER YOUR OPPONENT SCORES

When your opponent scores, it is possible to put the ball into play before the defense gets set. By having definite patterns, the offense can get the jump on the defense. In Diagram 17, the forwards break down court as soon as the opponents score.

X^1 takes the ball out of bounds as soon as your opponent scores and looks down court to see if X^4 or X^5 is loose. If X^1 spots either X^4 or X^5 free, he throws a long baseball pass. In the event he finds his forwards covered, he looks for his guards who are breaking in a pre-arranged pattern. Diagram 18 shows the position of the guards.

X^1 hits X^2 or X^3 on the sides whenever he cannot sight X^4 or X^5. X^1, the center, being near the basket on defense is the logical man to select to handle the ball out of bounds.

AFTER A REBOUND

As soon as you capture a rebound, it is possible to beat the defense down court before it is set. Diagram 19 shows how this break begins.

X^1 throws to X^2 or X^3 as soon as he gets the rebound, starting the break. In the event his forwards are covered, he seeks out his guards who break down court, either down the middle or down the sidelines. Diagram 20 shows how the four men break after the rebound.

X^1 hits X^4 or X^5 on the sides or down the middle to start off the break.

6

STYLES OF FAST
BREAK PLAY

THERE ARE THREE DIFFERENT STYLES OF FAST BREAKING NOW IN use: controlled fast break, fast break systems, and fire-horse basketball. Each style will be explained in detail below.

CONTROLLED FAST BREAK

Most teams use some form of controlled fast break. Whenever an opportunity presents itself to beat the defense down court, most teams today will take advantage of it. Diagram 21 shows how the defense will break after an intercepted pass.

Teams which include in their offensive repertoire breaking whenever such opportunities present themselves are said to be using a controlled break.

Dribbling and passing set up break. Some teams obtain offensive advantage through dribbling, others through passing. If a team has a good dribbler, it may take advantage of his ability by having him move down court whenever it has the ball. Meanwhile his team mates have outrun their guards to the forecourt. It is an easy matter for him to feed some team mate who is cutting for the basket. Other teams in similar situations will use the pass to get into the forecourt rapidly, thus initiating the break whenever they get the rebound and outnumber the defense.

DIFFERENT FAST BREAK SYSTEMS

Fast break systems originate from zone, man-to-man, and press. If a team bases its attack on definite fast break patterns

40

which the players practice daily, it uses a fast break system. These styles of breaking may originate from a zone defense, from a man-to-man defense, or from a press defense. No matter what the defense used may be, the offensive patterns do not vary. Hence, the term system.

ZONE FAST BREAK

Fast break pattern originates from 2-1-2 zone. In the following chapter we will cover in detail the various zone systems of breaking now in use. For our present purposes, we shall indicate how a fast break pattern may originate. Let us say that you are using a 2–1–2 zone defense. When your opponents shoot, miss, and you rebound, your players would set up a break as shown in Diagram 22.

MAN-TO-MAN FAST BREAK

Fast break may originate from a man-to-man defense. Although the defensive positions of the players using a man-to-man would not be the same as in a zone, the forwards would try to break to the sidelines. They could acomplish this by playing the offensive guards who bring the ball into the forecourt. As soon as the rebound is obtained, one forward would break to the right sideline and the other to the left sideline. The two players who do not get the rebound would cut down the center lane. Thus, in effect, the same result would be obtained. Diagram 23 illustrates this.

PRESS DEFENSE FAST BREAK

Press in forecourt causes bad passes. Some teams predicate their fast break on a press defense. The defense hounds the offense all over the court, forcing it to make all types of bad passes. As soon as a pass is stolen, the defense immediately shifts into offensive action. Each player runs to a definite spot, so that every player knows at all times where the other players should be. It is an easy matter then to drive for the basket, outnumbering and outspeeding the confused team. Diagram 24 shows how an intercepted pass is converted into a basket.

FIRE-HORSE BASKETBALL

To the uninitiated, fire-horse basketball appears to be a haphazard style of ball. As soon as possession is obtained, every player runs

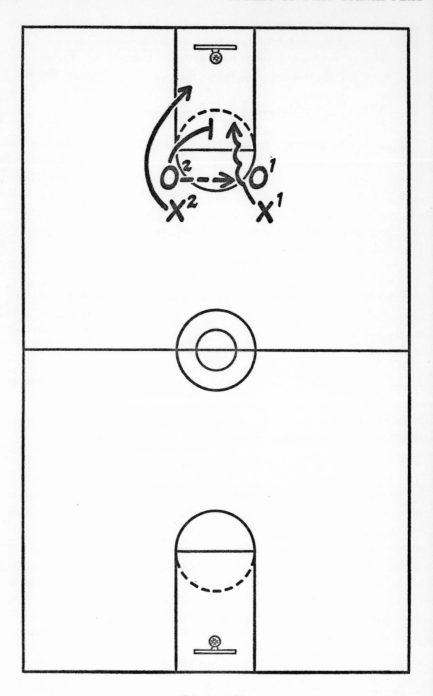

Diagram 21.

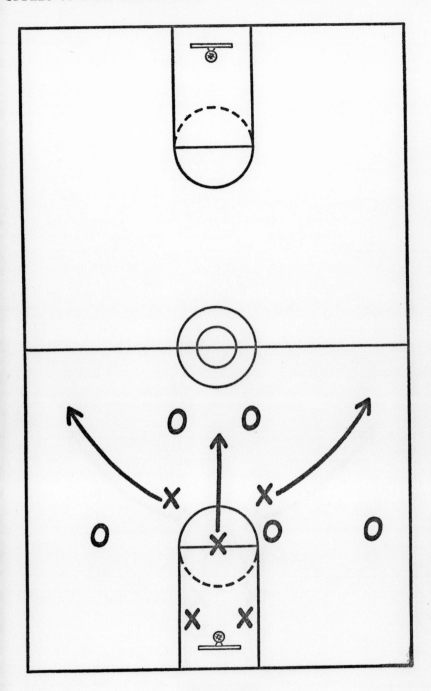

Diagram 22.

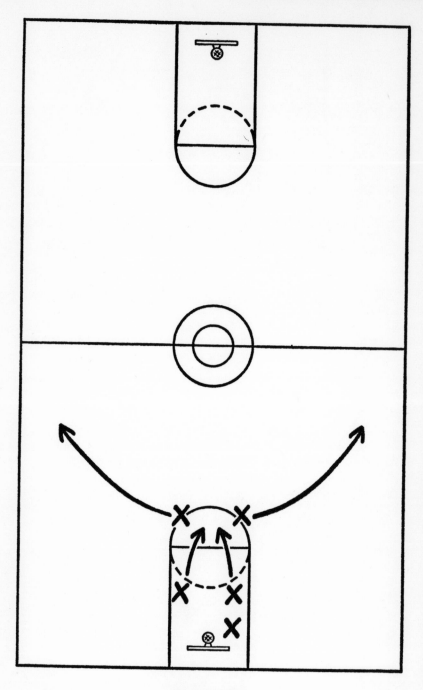

Diagram 23.

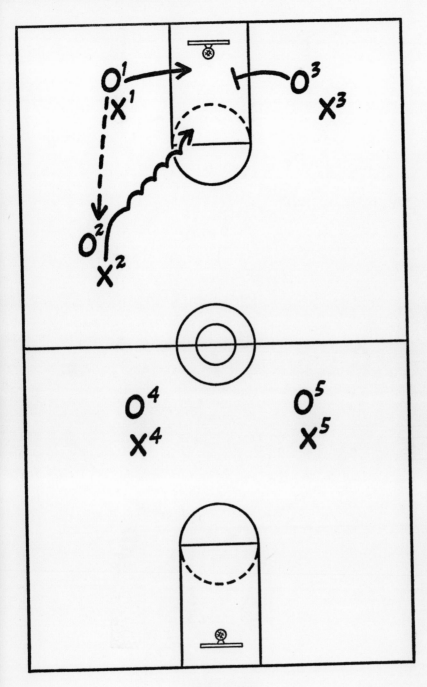

Diagram 24.

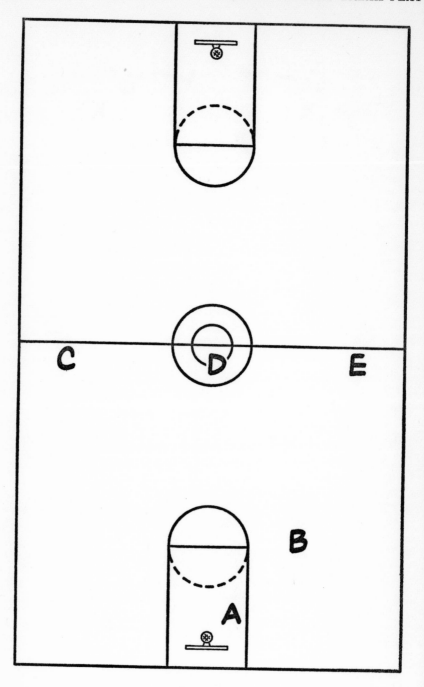

Diagram 25.

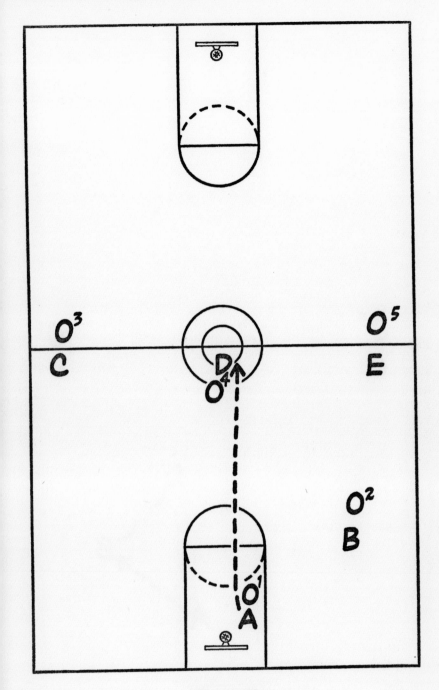

Diagram 26.

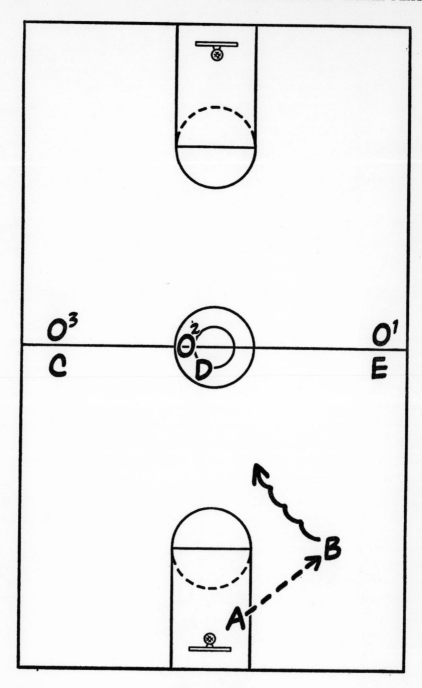

Diagram 27.

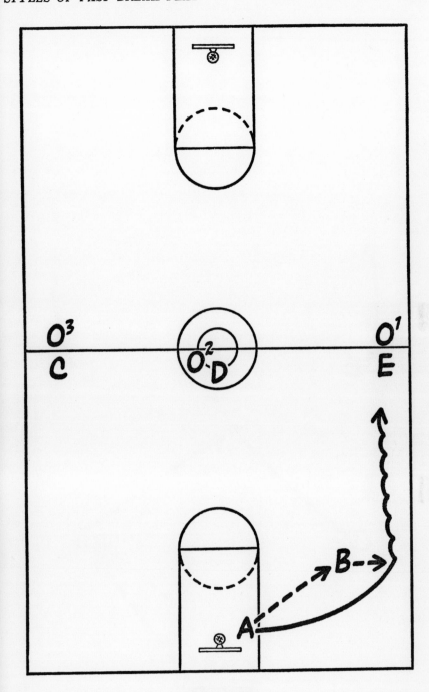

Diagram 28.

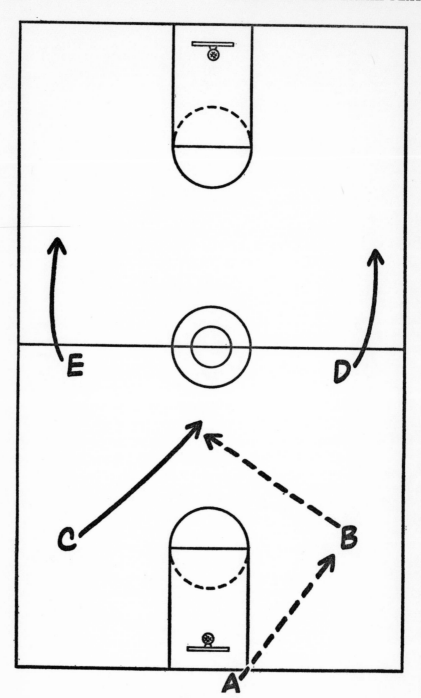

Diagram 29.

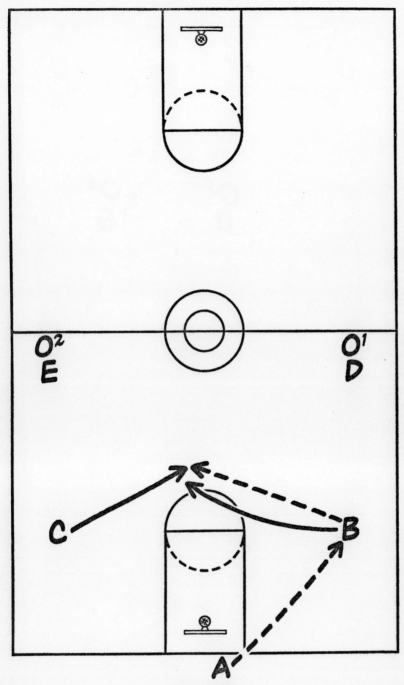

Diagram 30.

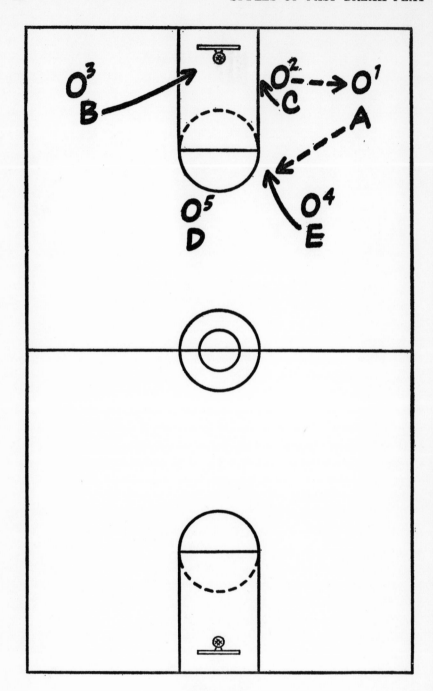

Diagram 31.

helter skelter towards the basket. When this style was first introduced by Frank Keaney of Rhode Island, every coach criticized it severely. It violated every known rule of good basketball—the long passes, the quick start down court, the quick hurried shots. But Keaney's phenomenal success with mediocre material soon convinced skeptics that it was not the helter skelter basketball found in Y.M.C.A.'s, but a well-organized style of fast breaking.

Fire-horse basketball wilts opponents. When Keaney wrote articles explaining his style and lectured at clinics, coaches realized that his patterns were based upon sound reasoning, although they were revolutionary. What appeared at first as foolish passes down court were in reality efforts to catch the defense napping. By selecting well-trained personnel, Keaney was able to outrun the defense and set up easy layups through long passes that pierced the defense.

Another aim of fire-horse basketball is to keep the defense moving at top speed at all times, so that it will wilt in the second half. Keaney's well-trained players would often catch much better and bigger clubs in the second half and beat them. In a National Invitation Tournament, a strong St. John's club literally buried a good Rhode Island team in the first half, gaining a 20 plus lead. No one in Madison Square Garden would have given a nickel for Rhode Island's chances in the second half. Yet in the second half Rhode Island ran St. John's into the ground for ten minutes, overcoming the deficit and going into the lead. It took a great strategic move on the part of St. John's to pull the game out of the fire. Their move will be considered in detail in Chapter 11. The pressure of moving at top speed at all times to prevent a rout soon will tell on the athlete who is not too well conditioned.

Well-conditioned players, quick passes, and fast shooting are needed. The main requisites of fire-horse basketball are well-conditioned players who are extremely fast, though not necessarily big; quick passes down court, and fast shooting. Only teams that possess these requisites are in a position to install fire-horse basketball. To achieve any degree of success in this style of ball, it is necessary to put in many, long hours of practice.

Rebounding initiates fire-horse basketball. Fire-horse basketball is put into practice in several ways. The most common way is through rebounding. After getting a rebound, the players move rapidly down court as shown in Diagram 25.

When A gets the rebound, he will look down court to see whether

C, D, or E has outrun his guards. If any one has done so, the pass is thrown to him. Let us say D has gotten the jump on his guard; the alignment of players will be thus as Diagram 26 shows.

Since only two guards can cover the three lanes, the break should result in an easy layup. The result would be the same if either C or E were open. Again there would be only two guards to cover three men.

If the three men down court were covered, the initial pass would go to B on the sideline. Diagram 27 shows the pattern of the break.

If B were covered, the break would follow the pattern illustrated by Diagram 28.

A would come around B to take the pass from B, and A's man would be run into B, thus liberating A for the break down court.

A second way of fire-horsing is to start the break immediately after the opposition scores. Diagram 29 demonstrates this.

A takes the ball out of bounds and throws to B. C moves to the center area to receive a pass from B. A three lane break is thus achieved.

A can initiate the break on the other side by throwing to C. In that event B would break into the center area to receive a pass from C. Again a three way break is achieved.

In the event C is covered by his opponent in the center area, he would pivot and give the ball to B who has followed his pass into the center area. Diagram 30 shows this maneuver.

Pressing in the backcourt. The third way to fire-horse is to press the opponents in the backcourt, forcing bad passes. As soon as a pass is intercepted, the break is on. Diagram 31 illustrates such a situation.

A intercepts the pass from O^2 and passes to E who cuts away from his guard the moment A obtains possession of the ball.

There are too many examples of teams using a controlled fast break to name them here, but we can mention an excellent example of a high school team using a quick break system.

A decade ago, Cliffside Park (New Jersey) High School used a three lane fast break to win the state title. With George Sella, who later became a Princeton great, in the middle lane on the quick break, Cliffside was able to swamp most of its opponents. Sella was the best example of how a player should manipulate the ball in the middle lane to draw defensive players out of position for scoring layups.

Sella was an excellent dribbler, and, through his individual brilliance, scored better than 20 points a game at a time when 10 points a game was considered an excellent night's work. He was also able to set up many scoring plays for his two forwards when the opposing guards covered him on the three lane break.

C.C.N.Y.'s cinderella team, which won the National Invitation and National Collegiate Athletic Association tournaments, also used a fast break system. They, however, used a man-to-man defense to set it up.

The best example of a high school fire-horse basketball team is Weehawken, New Jersey. Although Weehawken was a group II team, a school of some 700 students, it repeatedly defeated group IV teams, schools of 1500 or more students. During a 20 year period, meeting larger schools, Weehawken won more than 85% of its games. During the same period, against teams in its own class, Weehawken won 7 state championships and 12 sectional titles, not to mention countless county titles. Undoubtedly it was one of the most successful teams in the country, if not the most successful. What made the performance more remarkable is that the teams played in the hotbed of basketball—the New York Metropolitan area. They exemplified fire-horse basketball at its best.

Weehawken's college counterpart, Rhode Island, was the originator of fire-horse basketball. Rhode Island's success was phenomenal and they filled all the great arenas whenever they played. Playing against the leading colleges in the country, Rhode Island won about 80% of its games during a 5 year period. During this period, it received bids to the N.I.T. repeatedly, and its star center, Ernest Calverly, won All-American rating.

Introducing the baseball pass for the first time into basketball, Rhode Island made a shambles of all defenses. It was the first team to score in the 100's repeatedly. The remarkable part of its success was that it was accomplished with mediocre material. The tallest player was 6'2", and Calverly, at center, was a mere 5'10". Nothing can speak louder for fire-horse basketball than does the phenomenal success of Rhode Island.

7

HOW FAST BREAK PATTERNS OPERATE

Pattern BASKETBALL FROM THE FAST BREAK ARISES FROM EITHER a zone defense, a man-to-man defense, or a press defense.

Variety of zones used. Since it is much easier to break from the zone, most teams use this defense to set up their break. There are a variety of zones which are used for the break: 2–1–2, 2–3, 3–2, and 1–3–1.

FAST BREAKING FROM A 2–1–2

The position of your defensive players determines whether the break can be set up. The usual defensive alignment of the 2–1–2 is shown in Diagram 32.

Position of center, guards, and forwards. Your guards take their position about 3 feet in front of the opponent's basket, so that they can retrieve rebounds easily to set up the break. Your center takes his position in front of the free throw line. His position is the key one in the break. The forwards station themselves about eight feet in front of the free throw line, wating for the offense to come to them.

Guards must be tall and rugged. The guard retrieving the ball sets up the break. As soon as he gets the ball, he passes it to the sidelines to the forwards who are breaking down court. Thus the success of the break depends upon the guards who set it up. The guards must be good retrievers, tall and rugged.

Center must be a good all-around player. The center is the key man on offense. If he plays his position well, the break works; if not, it fails. The man selected for this position must be the fastest on the team; he must be a good dribbler, an excellent passer, and a good shot. In other words, he must be your best player. Although height is desirable, it is not all-important.

The forwards must be fast and excellent shots. It is also desirable that they dribble well to elude their opponents.

The guard starts the break. The break starts the moment that the guard releases the ball to the forward or the center who are breaking down court. The moment that he captures the rebound the forwards automatically run to the sidelines. The center drives down the middle lane, thus placing three offensive men on two defensive guards. Diagram 33 shows how the forwards and the center break down court.

The initial pass is made to spots to center or forward. When the guards retrieve the rebound, they release their passes to certain spots. The right guard releases it to the right forward on the sideline or to the center down the middle lane. The left guard releases his pass to the left forward or to the center. Let us say that your right guard has captured a rebound; his pass will be as shown in Diagram 34.

This pattern seems to be a very simple one, but you will find that it will be necessary for you to practice about a half hour daily to execute it properly.

You will find that your forwards will have difficulty in getting close to the sidelines to prevent the defensive guards from intercepting your guards' passes.

Forwards must go to the sidelines. In order to avoid this difficulty, have your forwards break slowly until they get close to the sideline and then break forward at top speed. This maneuver will prevent the defensive guards from getting too close to your forwards and from intercepting any passes. You cannot place too much stress on this drill.

Forward dribbles into opponent's forecourt on break. The moment that your forward receives the pass from the guard the break is on. Your forward dribbles as fast as he can, drawing the defensive guard to him, and then passes to the center. Your forward then breaks for the basket to receive a return pass from the center, if he is able to break away from his defensive guard. Diagram 35 illustrates this action.

Center is key man on three-lane break. The center, the most important "cog" in the three lane break, receives the pass usually from his forward after he has broken down court. When the forward is covered, the center receives the initial pass from the guard. After he receives the pass from the forward, the center continues dribbling towards the basket until he is covered by the defensive guard. Then he passes to whichever forward is free. If he is not covered, he dribbles in for a layup. Diagram 36 shows his position in the forecourt.

The defensive left guard has come over to cover the center who has passed to his offensive right forward. If the defensive right guard moves over to cover the center, the latter passes to his left forward as shown in Diagram 37.

The most difficult assignment your center must face occurs when the defensive guards retreat in such a way that they can watch your forwards and still cover the center. They accomplish this by remaining between the center and the forwards. It takes an excellent guard to do this. To find two guards who can play so well is a rare occurrence. However, when your center does encounter such a situation, he must be wily. Watching the guards warily, he drives in hard and shoots, trying hard for a rebound shot.

Set up drills to help center in game situations. You can readily see that the success of the three lane break depends upon your center's maneuvers. To help him meet the various situations that may arise in games, it is best for you to have drills in which the defensive guards vary their defensive maneuvers. At times, have the right guard cover the left forward; at other times, have him drift back cautiously. Have the left guard do the same. In other drills have the two guards retreat cautiously. The center must determine for himself, depending upon the situation arising, whether to shoot, pass, or drive in for a rebound.

Set defense is needed on the sides. This pattern is simple, although its execution is difficult at times because many defensive variations arise during the game. More problems arise when your opponents work the ball in at the sides. It will then be necessary for you to take the defensive alignment shown in Diagram 38.

2-1-2 becomes 3-2 on the sides. This defense really becomes a 3–2 on the sideline. (This position is necessary to prevent too many set shots.) Your center moves to the sideline to prevent a set shot. Your left guard moves over to the side, arms outstretched, to prevent a bounce pass to the player underneath. Your left forward moves over to the side, placing himself between the offensive forward and

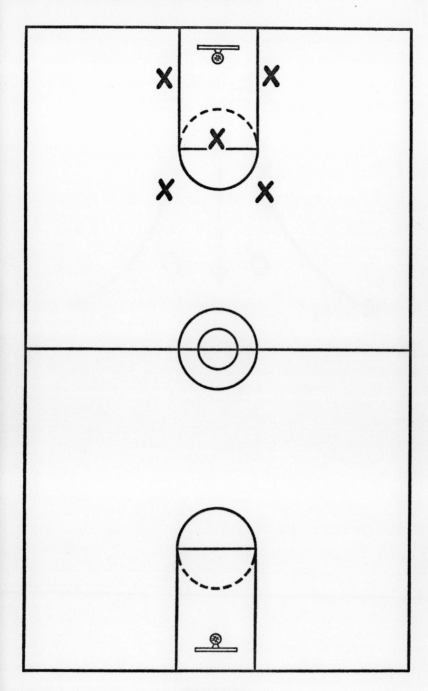

Diagram 32.

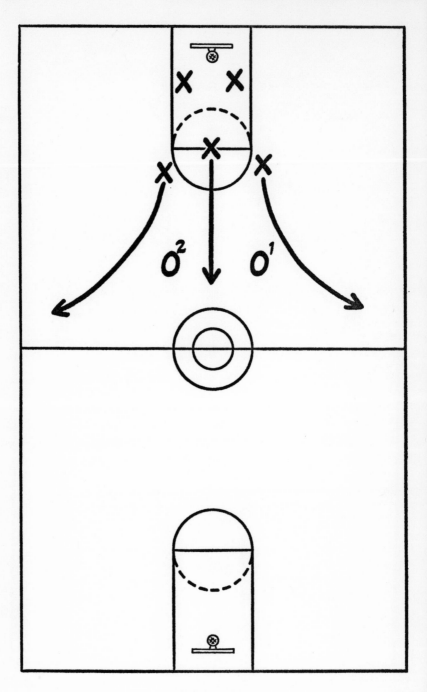

Diagram 33.

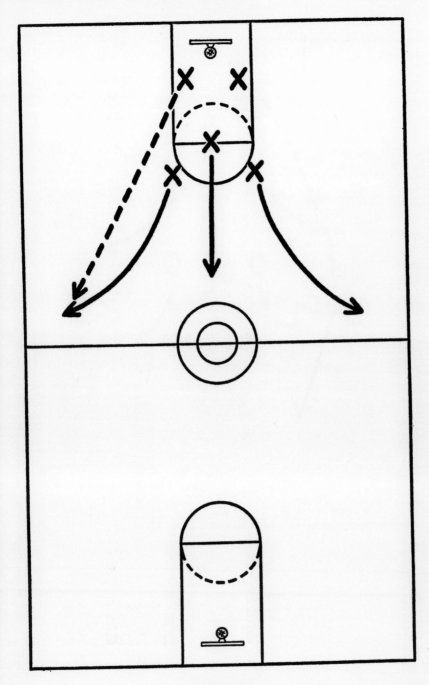

Diagram 34.

Diagram 35.

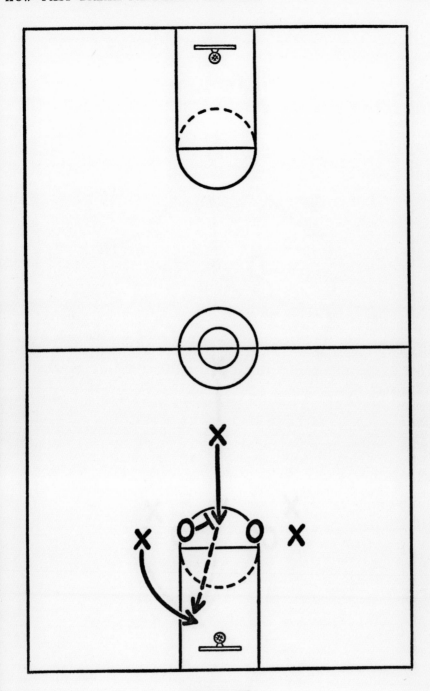

Diagram 36.

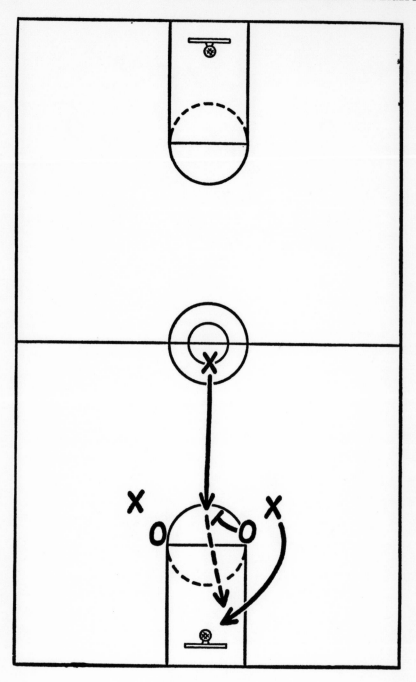

Diagram 37.

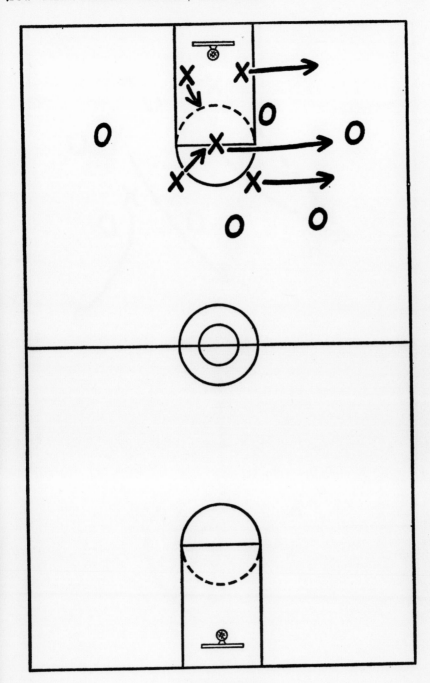

Diagram 38.

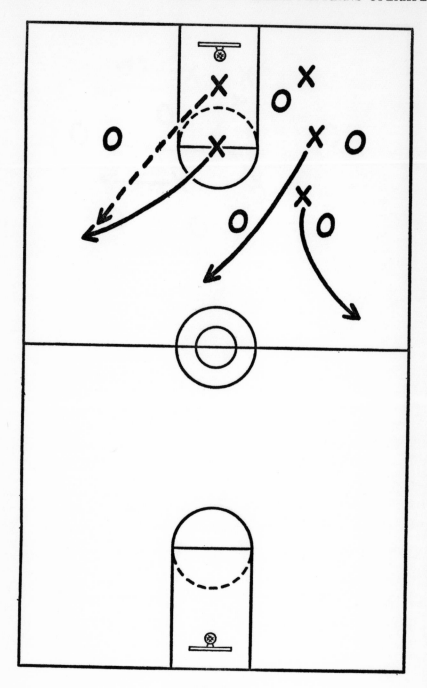

Diagram 39.

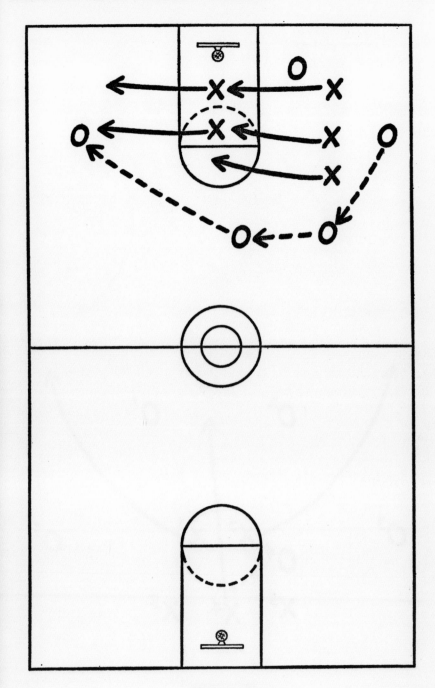

Diagram 40.

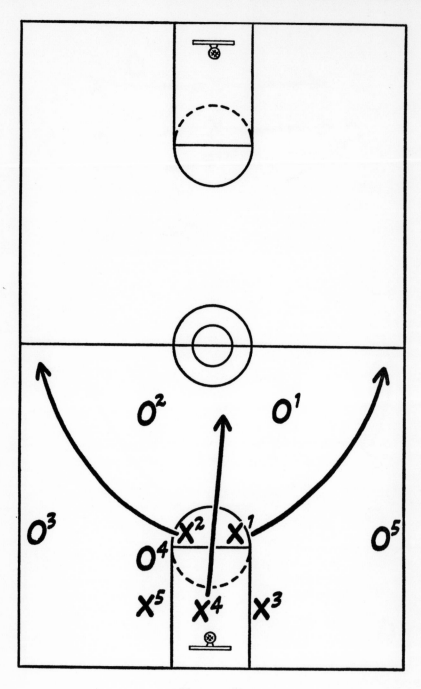

Diagram 41.

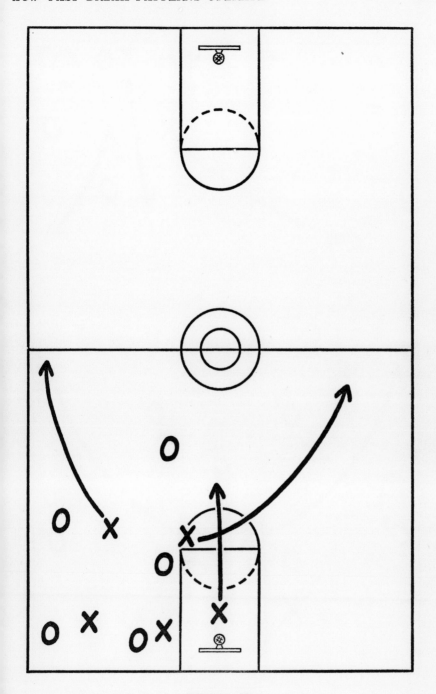

Diagram 42.

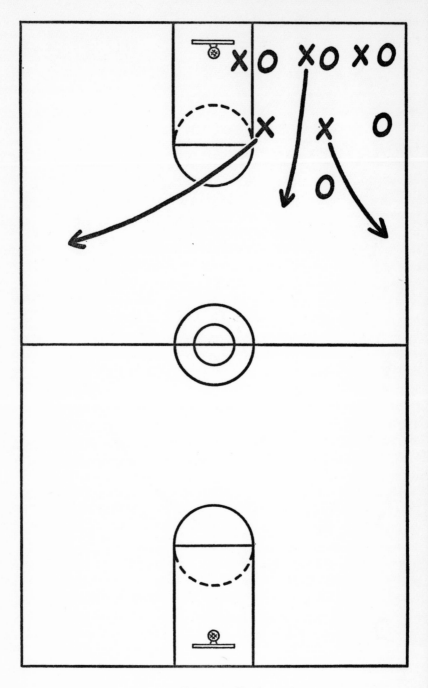

Diagram 43.

offensive guard, with outstretched arms, to prevent a return pass to the guard. Your right forward drops into the spot vacated by the center, bottling up the middle lane. The right guard moves forward into the free throw lane. From this position, your defense is set for interceptions. If the offense shoots, the zone is set for rebounds and fast breaking.

If the offensive forward shoots, the players will break as shown in Diagram 39.

Against a good passing team, forwards and center must cover openings. A good passing team will maneuver this defense out of position for scoring passes. When this situation arises, it is necessary for your forwards and your center to move over from their customary positions to cover openings. For example, let us take the following example: The offensive guard passes to his forward on the sideline, moving your defense to cover the area. The forward returns the pass to the guard who passes to the forward on the opposite sideline. This creates an opening because the center cannot move over to cover the forward. To cover this opening the right forward should move over to play the forward as Diagram 40 shows.

Your center moves over to his original position. Your right guard moves over to his original position. The left forward drops into the spot parallel to that of the right forward. The left guard moves in front of the basket. If the offensive forward shoots, your players are in a position to break for the basket.

FAST BREAKING FROM A 2–3 ZONE

Forwards move to sidelines on break. Another pattern of fast breaking takes place from a 2–3 zone. As in the 2–1–2 zone, the two front men break for the sidelines as soon as your opponent shoots. The right forward goes to the right sideline, and the left to the left sideline. When the rebound is captured, the center breaks down the middle lane as Diagram 41 shows.

Guards go down center lane when center rebounds. Whenever the center gets the rebound, he does not break down the middle lane; the left guard does so if he is free. If the left guard is out of position, the right guard goes down. Diagram 42 illustrates this break.

Guards take center's place in forecourt on break. When the guards receive the initial pass, they dribble down the center area until they are covered by a defensive player. Then they pass to the right forward who continues down court until covered by a defensive player. The forward then passes back to the center area; the guard drives in for the shot if he is free, or passes to the left forward.

The break down court may be difficult when the offense spreads your defense; nevertheless, the break still can take place. Diagram 43 shows how the players break when these conditions occur.

Your left forward breaks to the left sideline. Your right forward has more ground to cover to reach the right sideline. Your center has little difficulty in going down the center lane. The right guard initiates the break with a pass to the center or the right forward.

Defense must maintain positions to rebound. The defense must keep in mind that it has to maintain its defensive position to get rebounds; otherwise, there will be no fast break opportunities. Therefore, it is important to keep one man under the basket for rebounding. If the defense is straddled to the right, the left guard will be under the basket. The reverse is true when the defense is straddled to the left.

Weakness of 2-3 zone is at the sides. The greatest weakness of this zone is at the sides. If the opponents riddle your defense, the fast break stalls. Therefore, it is necessary for you to have your players move rapidly on defense to keep the offense off balance.

FAST BREAKING FROM A 3–2 ZONE

Three front men on 3-2 zone break into forecourt. The 3–2 zone is the best for fast breaking, since the offense is geared for quick breaks down court with the three front men. Unless the offensive team keeps three men back on offense, the moment it loses the ball it finds itself outnumbered 3–2 as the three front men break into forecourt. If it does keep three men back on offense, it will have no offense. Thus it is faced with the dilemma of either having no offense or weakening its defense. Diagram 44 shows the offensive break of the three front men.

The defense will encounter more difficulty when your opponents work the ball in on the sides. Diagram 45 shows the offensive moves of the players.

The right forward will find it difficult to break to the right sideline as he is too far over, but he can make up some of this distance by breaking as soon as your opponent shoots.

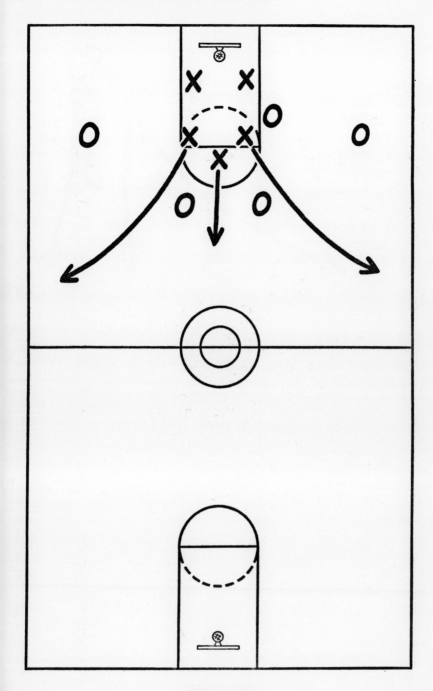

Diagram 44.

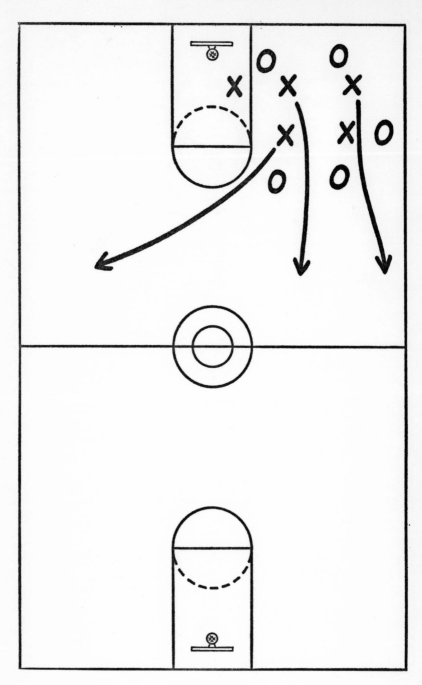

Diagram 45.

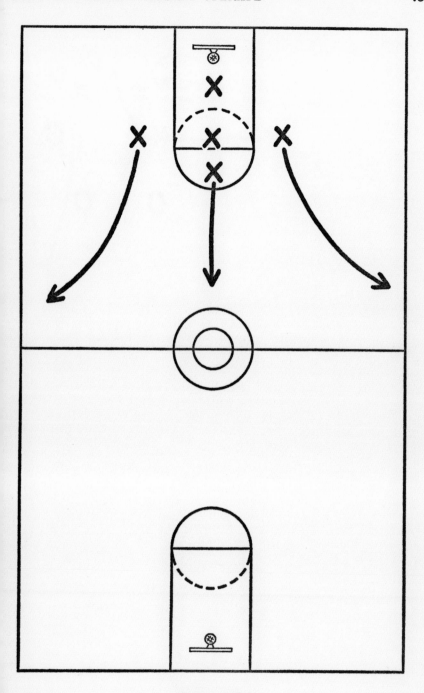

Diagram 46.

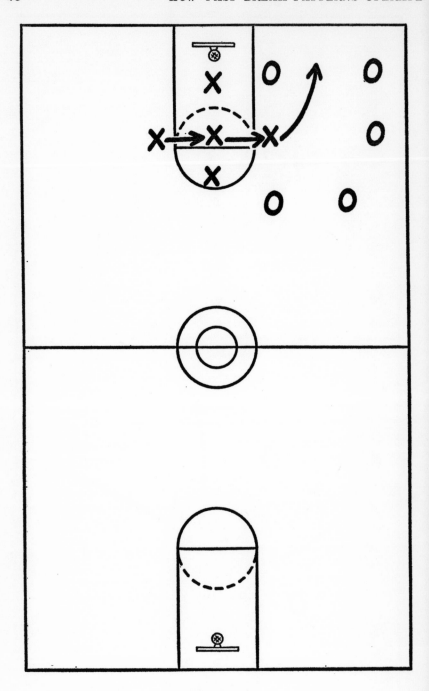

Diagram 47.

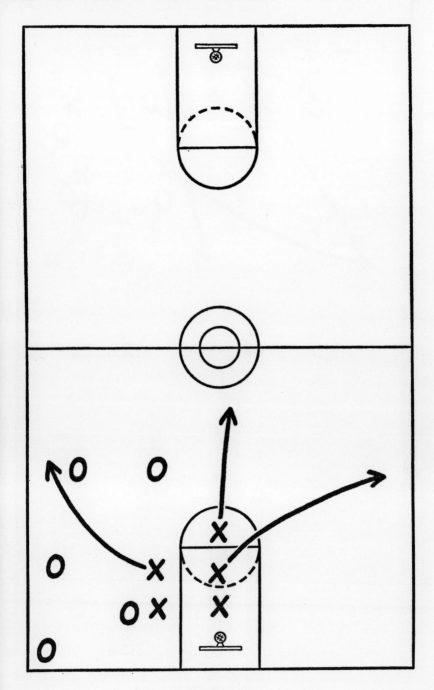

Diagram 48.

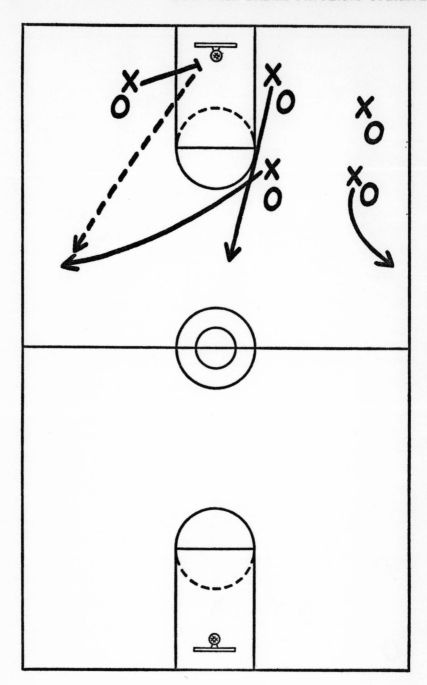

Diagram 49.

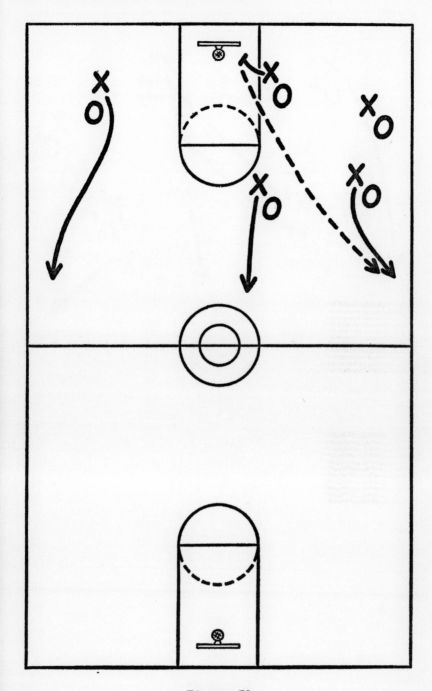

Diagram 50.

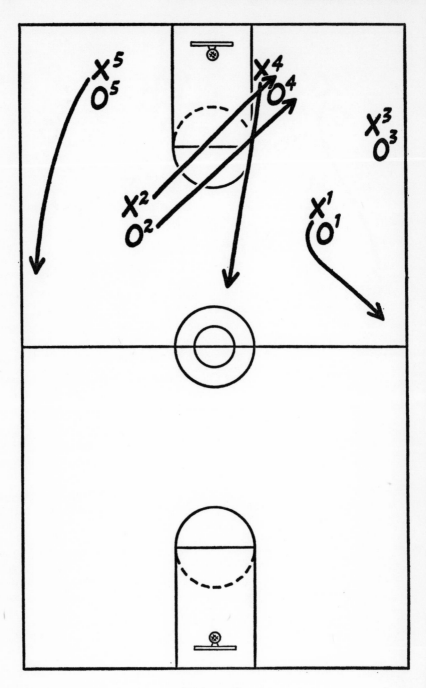

Diagram 51.

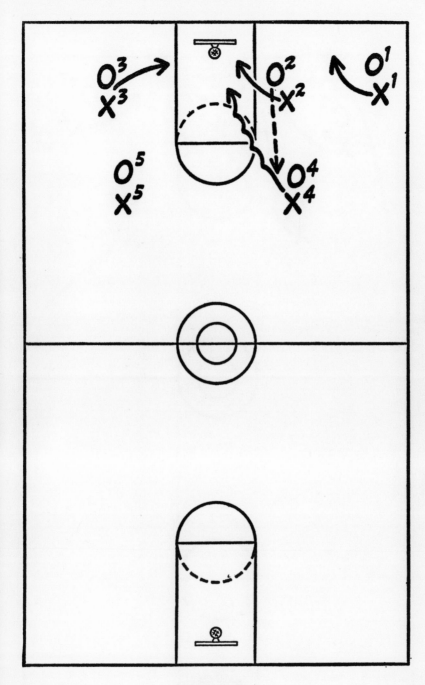

Diagram 52.

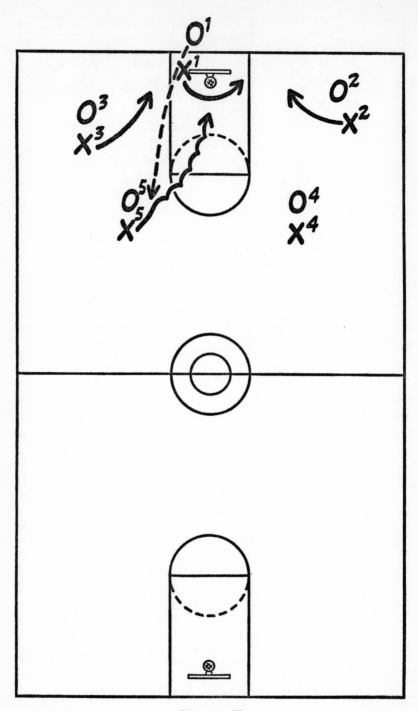

Diagram 53.

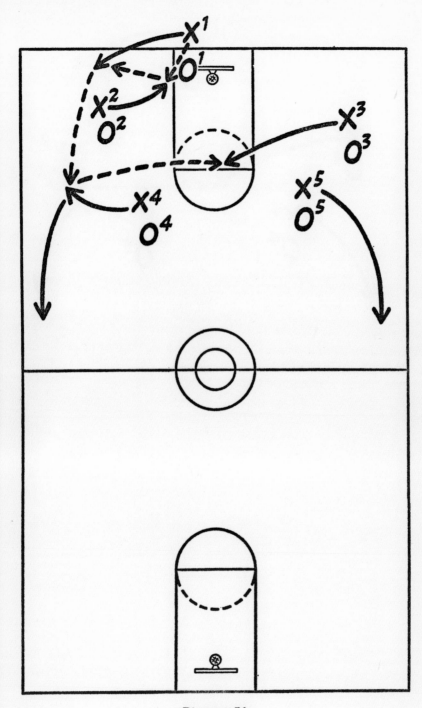

Diagram 54.

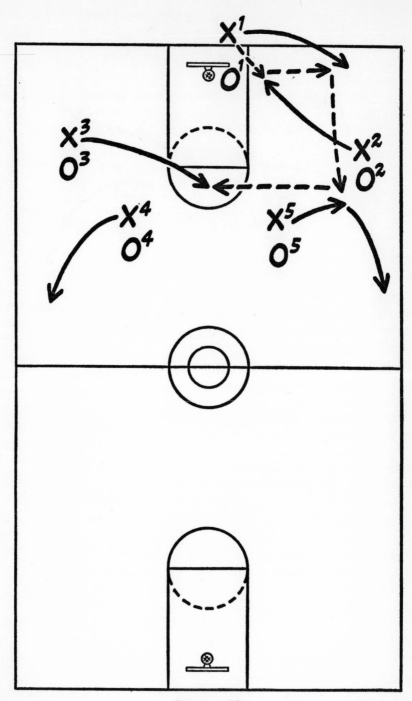

Diagram 55.

FAST BREAKING FROM THE 1-3-1 ZONE

Break from 1-3-1 zone is not too effective. The break from this zone is not as effective as it is from the 2–1–2 or 3–2 because the second line of defense is farther back. Nevertheless, you can break from this defense. Diagram 46 shows the path of breaking of the players.

When your opponents work the ball in at the sides, the defense becomes a 2–3 zone as Diagram 47 shows.

Diagram 48 shows how the break takes place from this defense. As you can see, the break is very similar to that of the 3–2.

FAST BREAKING FROM A MAN-TO-MAN DEFENSE

Breaking from man-to-man defense is difficult. Since the players are not in the same position as they would be in the zone, the break from man-to-man defenses is more difficult. Nevertheless, through much practice, forwards can learn to break to the sidelines as they do in the zone defense. No matter where they are, they will have the jump on the guards and the center because they will be outside more as the opposing guards usually play outside. Diagram 49 shows a situation that may arise when the guards have not cut in for shots.

As the diagram shows, the forwards break for the sidelines and the center goes down the middle lane. If the center rebounds, as often happens, the right guard will go down the sideline. The right forward would go down the center lane, and the left forward to the left sideline. Diagram 50 illustrates this.

The most difficult type of break, of course, is when the guards cut in on offense. Diagram 51 sets up a situation that arises after a screen.

Three-lane break arises from shot missed. The left guard, O^2, has cut to his right and has run his defensive forward into the screen. O^2 has shot and missed. The offensive break is the same as it was in the above illustration, because the defensive right forward, X^2, goes down the middle. The defensive right guard, X^5, goes down the right side. Of course, the left forward goes down the left side. Thus, a three lane break is effected. No defense can stop this break unless it keeps three men back on offense. As we pointed out before, any team that does that will have no offense.

FAST BREAKING FROM A PRESS DEFENSE

Break takes place in opponent's forecourt. The half-court press and the full-court press have definite patterns for fast breaking. In the full-court press, the break often occurs in the opponent's backcourt (your forecourt,) since interceptions take place there. Diagram 52 sets up the following situation.

X^4 intercepts O^{2}'s pass. He dribbles downcourt. If O^2 covers X^2, X^4 dribbles in for the shot. O^2 covers X^4, the latter passes to X^2, who moves to the basket.

Diagram 53 sets up a pass interception from an out-of-bounds.

X^5 intercepts O^{1}'s long pass and dribbles down the center lane. As O^1 moves in to cover him, X^1 moves to the right side to receive a pass from X^5. If O^2 or O^3 move over to cover X^5, he passes to X^2 or X^3 under the basket.

FAST BREAKING AGAINST A PRESS DEFENSE

Press defense is wide open for fast breaking. One of the most unusual breaks is that against a press defense. When a team uses a full court press, it leaves itself wide open for fast breaking. Against a back court press, the following patterns will lead to quick break baskets. Diagram 54 shows this.

X^1 throws to X^2 who has come over to receive the out-of-bounds pass. X^2 throws it back to X^1 at his left side. Meanwhile X^4 has gone to the left sideline to receive X^{1}'s pass. X^4 passes to X^3 who has broken down the center lane. X^5 goes down his sideline. X^4 does the same on his side. Thus, a three lane break is effected against this backcourt press.

Diagram 55 shows how this same pattern operates on the other side. X^1 passes to X^3 who passes back to X^1. X^1 passes to X^5 who has gone to the right sideline to receive X^{5}'s pass. X^4 goes down the left sideline and X^5 down the right side. Once again a three lane break is effected.

A few examples illustrating how the various fast break defenses operate would be appropriate here. In a state tournament game, Glassboro, New Jersey, High School, using a 2–1–2 zone, was able to capitalize on its defensive rebounding by setting up many quick breaks. Glassboro had a good middle man who set up many layup scoring plays. Its opponent, Cape May, noticing the weakness on the sides, exploited it throughout the game to keep it in contention.

Cape May had two excellent shots who scored repeatedly from the sides. Anderson, who later played end for the New York football Giants, was an excellent rebounder, and he controlled the defensive boards so that Glassboro had to score consistently on its fast breaks to avoid losing the ball. In one of the best and closest games played in the state tournament, Cape May went on to win its twentieth straight game because it was able to exploit the weakness of the 2–1–2 zone.

In a New York Section III game against Richfield Springs, Canastota High School used a 2–3 zone effectively for its quick break. Every opportunity it had after a rebound, Canastota would fast break, scoring on easy layups, overwhelming its opponent. In this game, the power of the quick break was in evidence because Canastota could control the boards.

In a later game in the same tournament, Hamilton High School was able to exploit the defensive weakness of the 2–3 on the sides, often maneuvering the two front men out of position to score on set shots. However, Canastota capitalized on every fast break opportunity to win decisively, thus winning the title.

Corpus Christi High School, Galesburg, Illinois, used a press defense to set up fast breaks throughout the 1948 Christmas tournament to defeat superior opponents. Having small but fast men, Corpus Christi utilized every ounce of ability to hound its opponents all over the court, with the result it completely demoralized them. The strength of the press as a quick break defense was never more in evidence than in the finals of this tournament. Corpus Christi averaged 5'9" to its opponent's 6'2", yet the press caused the opponents to make many bad passes which were intercepted for easy layups.

8

BLENDING A FAST BREAK
WITH A DELIBERATE PLAY

During the game many occasions will arise when it is not possible for you to fast break. Your opponents may use delaying tactics, may crowd the rebounder, or may press in the back court. In each case, it is necessary that you use deliberate plays. A good team must be able to blend its deliberate patterns with its fast break. The deliberate plays selected must depend on the personnel available; the specific defense used will also help determine the type of plays selected.

You must decide to use the single pivot as the basis of your deliberate plays. Any team using a three lane break can very easily use a single pivot, since the center goes down the middle lane and the forwards to the sides. When the break stalls, the center automatically finds himself in the pivot post and the forwards on the side. From this position, pivot plays can be initiated. A simple play is a screen off the pivot by the forwards as shown in Diagram 56.

X^2 passes to the center X^1 and goes past him, hoping to drive his guard into X^1. If that fails, X^3 drives past X^1 for a possible screen. If timed properly, either X^2 or X^3 will be free for a shot.

Another possible screen off the pivot is set up by the guards, X^4 and X^5. Diagram 57 illustrates this maneuver.

X^4 passes to X^1 and cuts past him. X^5 drives in on the other side. One of the two should get loose, since X^4 or X^5's guards will be picked off.

Another screen off the pivot is started by X^4. He dribbles to X^2 and passes to him. X^2 dribbles past X^1, screening off O^2. See Diagram 58.

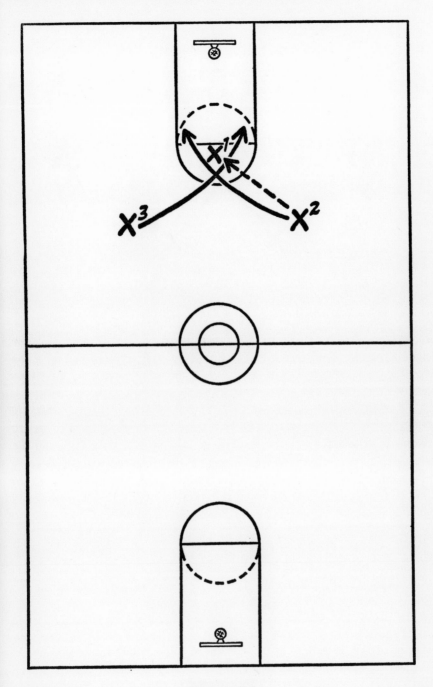

Diagram 56.

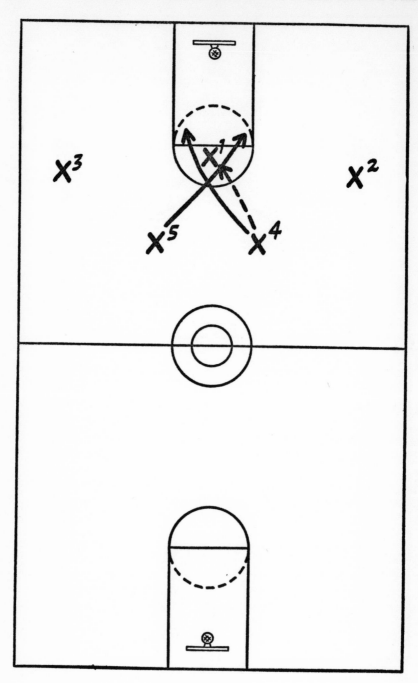

Diagram 57.

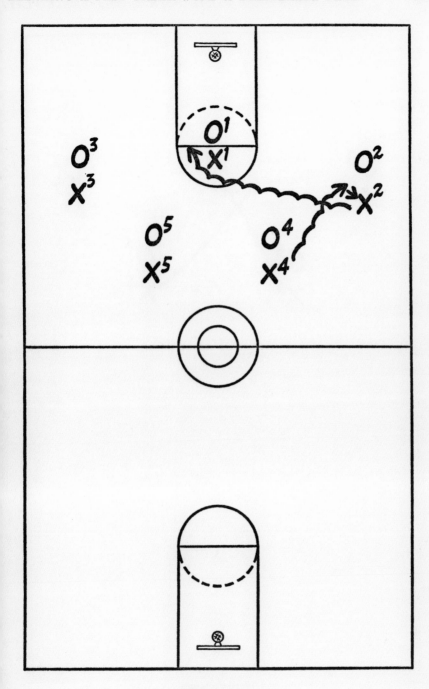

Diagram 58.

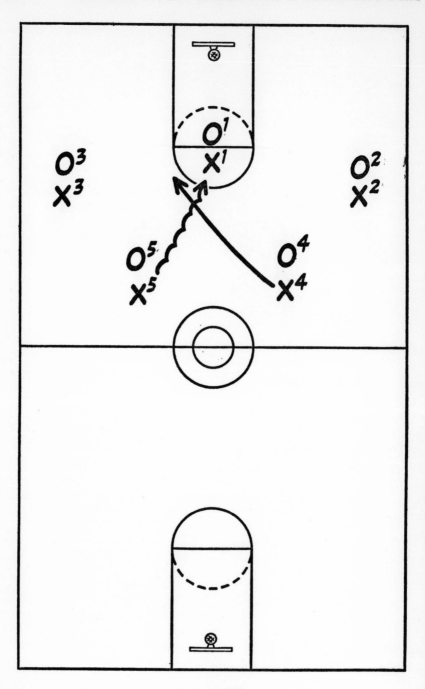

Diagram 59.

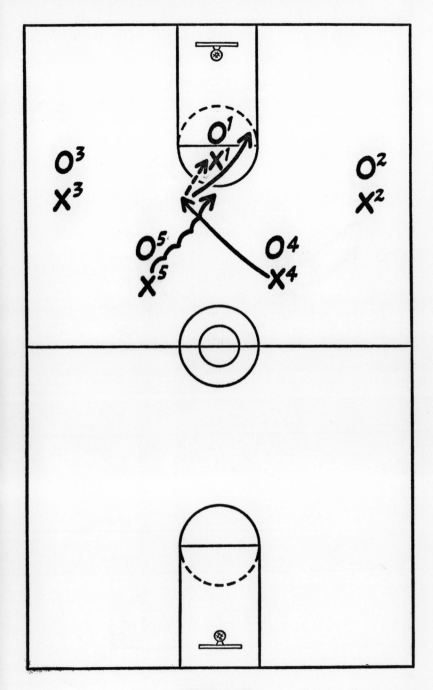

Diagram 60.

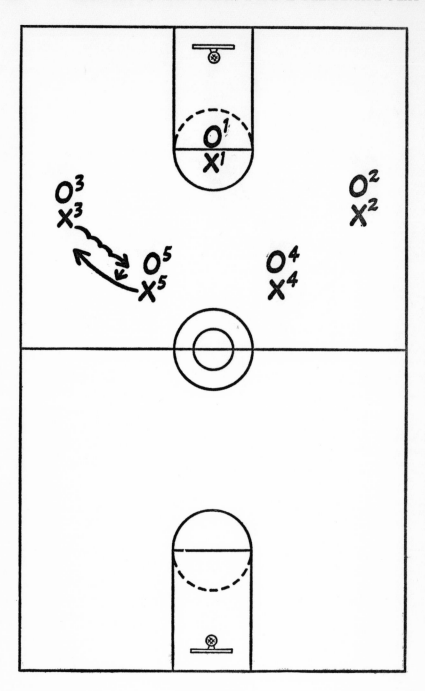

Diagram 61.

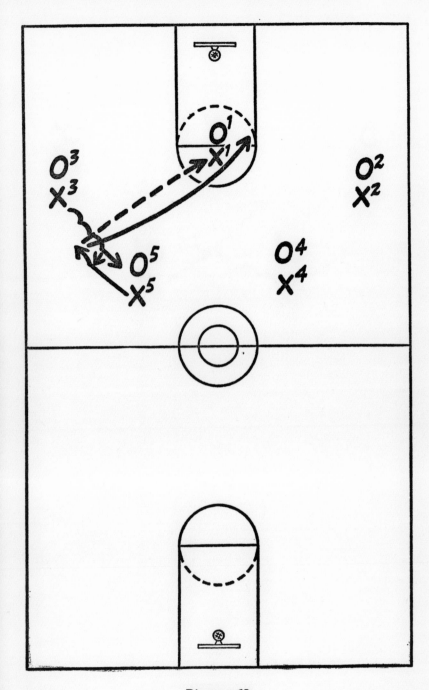

Diagram 62.

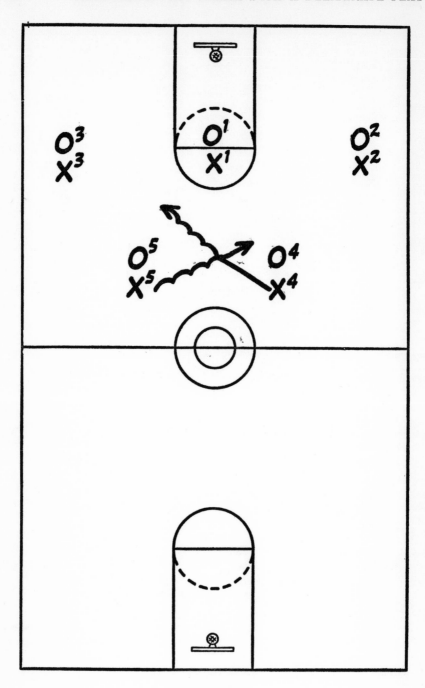

Diagram 63.

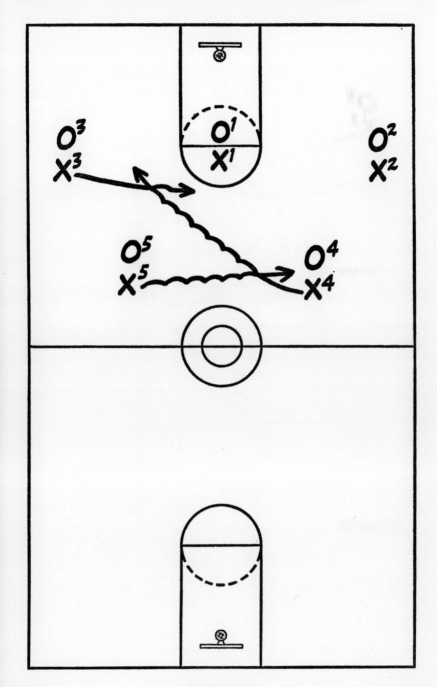

Diagram 64.

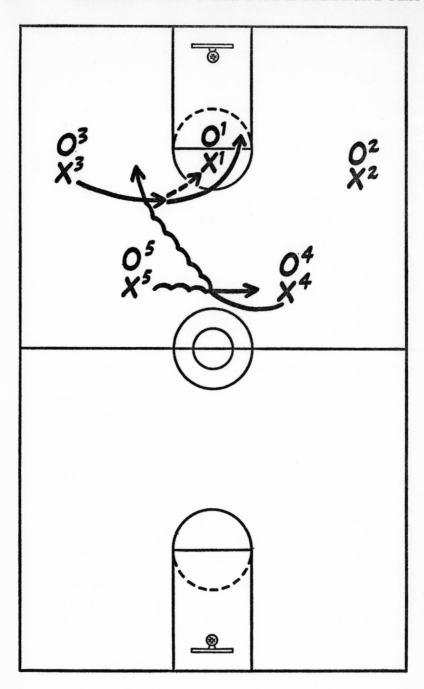

Diagram 65.

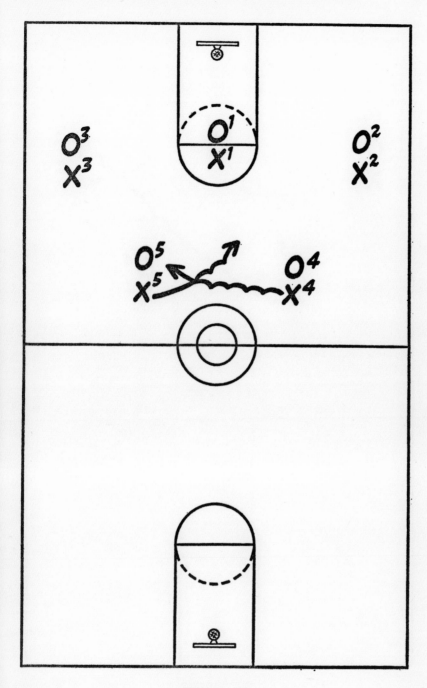

Diagram 66.

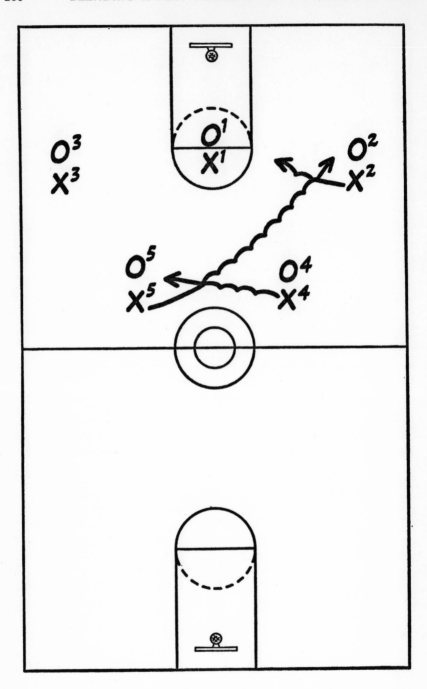

Diagram 67.

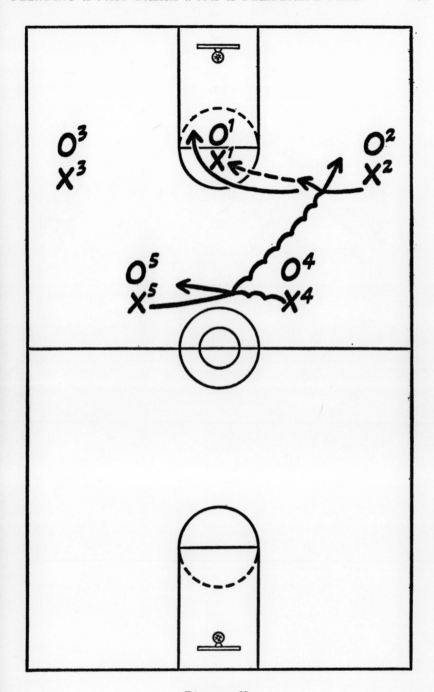

Diagram 68.

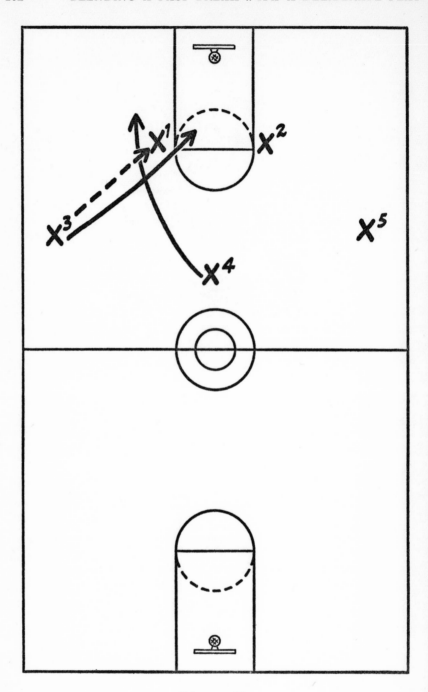

Diagram 69.

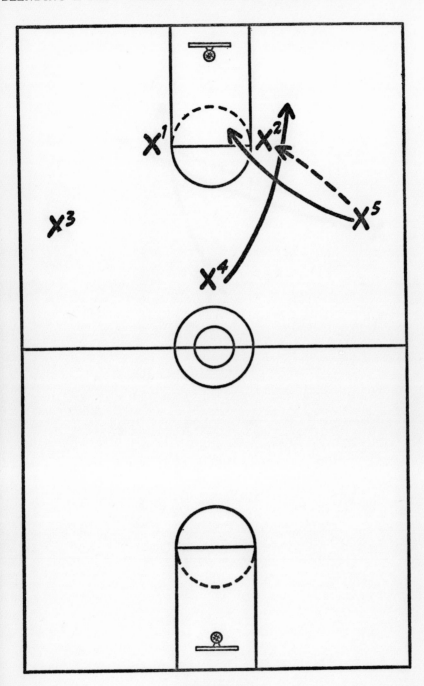

Diagram 70.

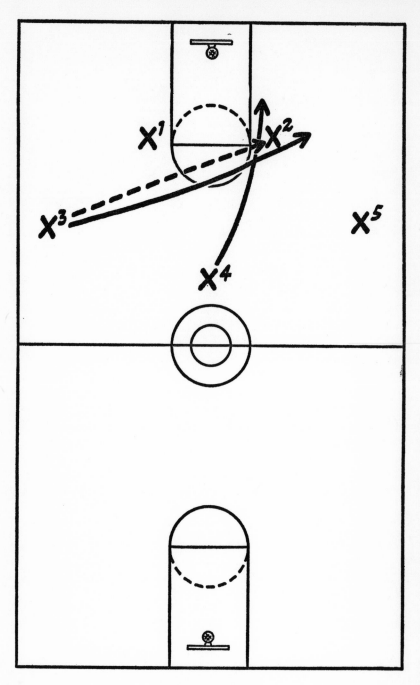

Diagram 71.

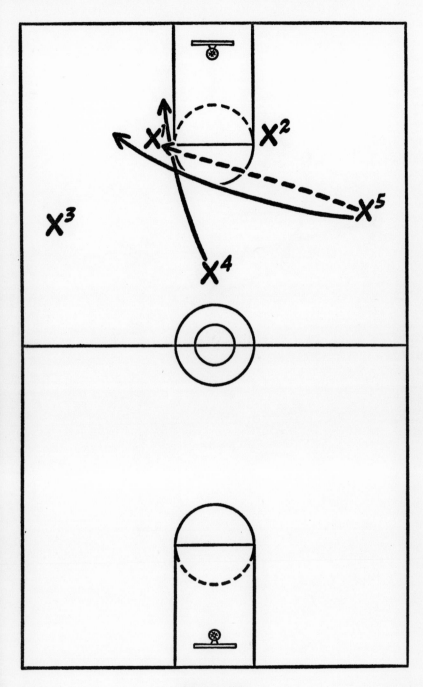

Diagram 72.

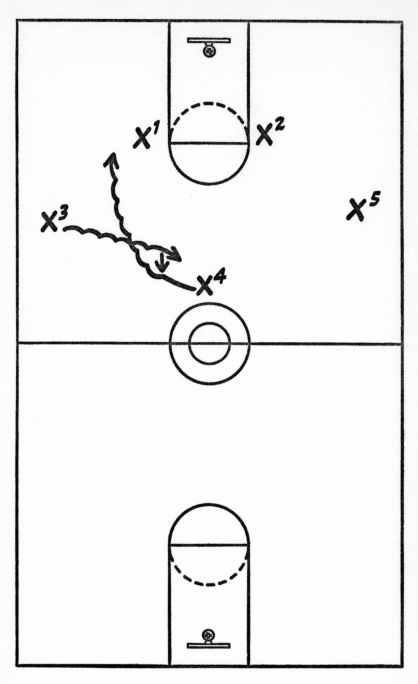

Diagram 73.

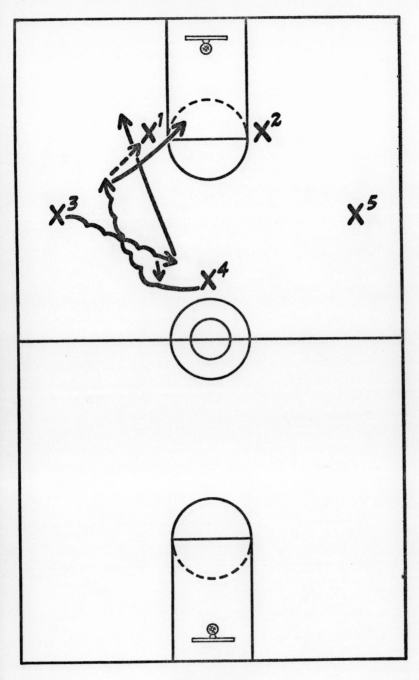

Diagram 74.

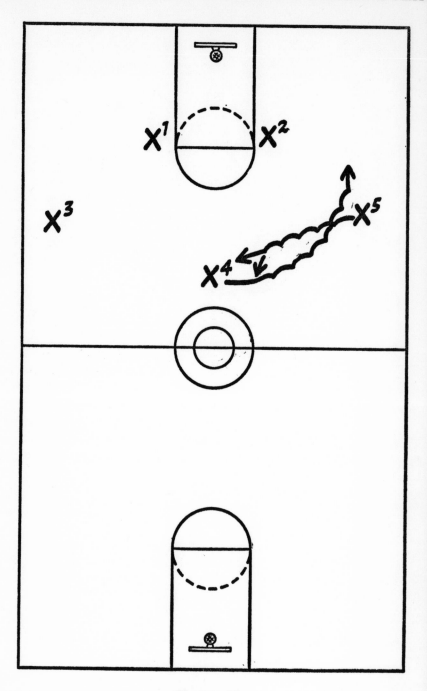

Diagram 75.

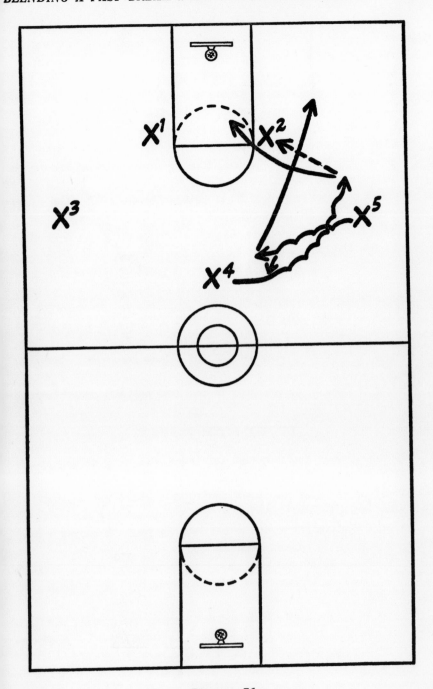

Diagram 76.

X^2 may get a screen off X^4. If not, he may get it off X^1. If X^2 does not get the screen off X^4, he may pass in to X^1 and drive past him.

X^5 may initiate a screen by dribbling towards X^1. X^4 cuts off X^5, hoping to screen off his guard. See Diagram 59.

If X^4 fails to get loose, he passes in to X^1 and cuts past him. He should screen off his guard here. See Diagram 60.

X^3 can initiate the screen by dribbling towards X^5. The latter drives off X^3. See Diagram 61.

If he can get loose, he drives in. If not he passes in to X^1 and drives past him. See Diagram 62.

Another possibility is for X^5 to dribble towards X^4. The latter drives off X^5. See Diagram 63.

If X^4 is loose, he dribbles in. If not, X^3 drives off X^4 for a possible screen. See Diagram 64.

Failing in this, X^3 passes in to X^1 for a possible screen. See Diagram 65.

X^4 can initiate the same pattern on the other side. In this case, X^4 dribbles toward X^5. The latter drives off X^4 for a possible screen. See Diagram 66.

Failing in this, X^2 drives past X^5 for a possible screen. See Diagram 67.

Failing in this, X^2 passes in to X^1 and cuts past him. See Diagram 68.

DOUBLE PIVOT PLAYS

Depending upon the material available, you may decide to use a double pivot as the basis of your deliberate plays. In that case, the center would play one pivot post and a guard the other pivot. When the break fails to materialize, it will be necessary to slow down sufficiently to allow the guard to get into the post. A simple screen from this offense is seen in Diagram 69.

X^3 passes in to X^1 and cuts past him, hoping to get a screen off X^1. If this fails, X^4 cuts past X^1. A screen may arise from this double cut.

X^5 may initiate a screen from the double pivot by passing in to X^2. He cuts past X^2. If a screen fails here, X^4 cuts past X^2. A screen should arise from this double cut. See Diagram 70.

Another pattern from the double pivot arises when X^3 passes in to X^2. He cuts past him to get a screen on his guard. If he fails in this, X^4 cuts inside X^2. See Diagram 71.

X^5 may start a similar pattern on the left pivot X^1 by passing to him and cutting outside of him. If he fails to screen off his guard, X^4 cuts inside of X^1. See Diagram 72.

X^3 may originate a double pivot pattern by dribbling and passing to X^4 who cuts outside of X^3. See Diagram 73.

If a screen fails, X^4 passes in to X^1 and cuts inside of X^1 while X^3 cuts outside of him. See Diagram 74.

X^5 may originate a similar continuity on the right side. X^5 dribbles and passes to X^4 who cuts past him. See Diagram 75.

Failing in this screen, X^4 passes in to X^2. X^4 cuts inside of X^2 while X^5 cuts outside of X^2. This double pincer may lead to a screen for either X^4 or X^5. See Diagram 76.

Georgia Military College is an example of a team blending its deliberate patterns well with the fast break. Breaking from both a zone and a man-to-man, it used a single pivot for its deliberate plays when the break stalled. When it broke from a zone, it would send its center down the middle. Failing to obtain an advantage of numbers on the break, it immediately went into a pattern of deliberate continuities based on a single pivot. The forwards on the sides would set up pivot screens, running opposing guards into the post. If they failed, or for variety, the guards would try to screen off their opponents.

Blending the fast break well with the deliberate patterns, this small college in 1953 turned out its best team in 15 years; one of the best teams in Georgia among small colleges.

9

DEFENSES FOR FAST BREAK BASKETBALL

ANY OFFENSIVE TEAM MUST HAVE AN ADEQUATE DEFENSE IF IT expects to be successful. What good is it if you score 100 points a game when your opponents score 105? The Boston Celtics for years had the best offensive team in professional basketball, but the worst defense. The result was that Boston did not win any championships until it acquired Bill Russell, the defensive specialist from the national college champions, St. Francisco University. Russell strengthened Boston's defense one hundred per cent.

A fast break team must decide what defense to use and which one will best suit its personnel. The various defenses found are described below.

MAN-TO-MAN DEFENSE

Man-to-man defense is the best defensively. The best defense to use when a team has many good guards is a man-to-man. A good man-to-man assures the team defensive balance. It need not fear weaknesses which can be exploited in other defenses. However, a man-to-man defense greatly limits the offense. Since fast break patterns cannot be set up too easily, the average team may experience difficulty in installing the break. Another difficulty is that it takes a much longer time to set up a fast break system. Since a defensive player may not be in position to break when his teammates get the rebound, the break is often haphazard. However, through constant drilling, a fairly successful break can be worked out.

ZONE

Zone is weak defense. The zone is considered weak by some coaches, but it may be necessary to use the zone because a team has poor guards. A team may decide to use the zone because it has tall guards who rebound well. When a team has tall players who are awkward or who can easily be feinted out of position, it is better to use a zone.

Zone is best for fast breaking. Offensively, the zone defense is the best one to use for fast breaking, since the players are always in certain prearranged positions from which they can break. The players, knowing where each member is, can initiate the break without any hesitation by making the all-important first pass.

2-1-2 ZONE

The 2-1-2 zone. The type of zone selected will depend on the personnel. If a team has only two good rebounders, it would be better to use a 2–1–2 zone. By placing these two guards near the basket, the team will be assured of capturing a fair share of rebounds. Through rebounding, you will be able to fast break.

Forwards stop set shots. Forwards play some eight feet in front of the foul line, stopping outside shooting. They move out more when an opponent shoots well from outside. The two forwards should complement each other. If the opponents have one good outside shot and one weak one, the two forwards play closer to the good shot.

Middle man must be fast. The middle man in this defense has to cover both sidelines for set shooting. Hence, he should be a fast man, able to maneuver from side to side to prevent shots. He should also cover the front apex of the defensive triangle around the basket. See Diagram 77.

This defense is weak at the sides. Weaknesses of this defense are quite obvious. It is weak at the sides. Any good set-shooting team will out-maneuver the defense to take scoring shots.

Offensively, its strength lies in its position. As soon as a team gets a rebound, it is in a position to set up a three lane break. The front men will be in offensive territory before the defense can set itself.

3–2 ZONE

As is the case in the 2–1–2, this zone has the best rebounders near the basket. Their task is the same: to control the boards. The middle man of the 2–1–2 plays up front in the 3–2. He plays a little ahead of the forwards, some eight feet ahead of the foul line. The forwards play to the left and to the right of the middle man. See Diagram 78.

Middle man plays front men. The middle man on the 3–2 plays everything up front. The forwards play the sides. When the ball goes to the sides, the middle man drops inside the foul line. The forward opposite the ball drops inside as Diagram 79 shows.

The weakness of this zone lies in the corners. A good corner shot can riddle this defense. Its strength is on the offense. The moment the team obtains the ball it has three men downcourt to place great pressure on the defense.

3-2 is good for fast breaking. If a team is limited in rebound men and has an abundance of fast men, the 3–2 is an excellent defense to use to set up the fast break.

2–3 ZONE

2-3 is strong defensive zone. When a team has an abundance of good rebounders, a 2–3 zone is a good one to use. This zone is very strong for rebounding because it has continually an apex of defense around the basket. The guards play a little further out so that they can prevent corner shooting. The middle man of the 2–1–2 is directly in front of the basket. In the 2–3 he should be the best rebounder. Usually he is the tallest man on the team.

Forwards must cover the sides. The forwards in the 2–3 are not only responsible for the front men but must also cover the sides. When the ball is on the sides, one forward drops into the foul area to protect it. See Diagram 80.

Weakness of zone lies at the sides. The weakness of this zone lies at the sides. Two forwards find it very difficult to cover three men. Hence, side shooting often ruins a 2–3 zone. However, it is possible to decrease this weakness by having one of the guards cover the side. See Diagram 81.

This zone offensively is not as strong as the 2–1–2 or 3–2 because it has only two men up front. On a break, one of the three back men must go down the middle lane. Since he is quite a distance back, the defense has time to set itself up.

1-3-1 ZONE

1-3-1 is strong on sides and under the basket. When a team has a tall, exceptional rebounder, it may decide to use a 1–3–1 zone. If a team has only one good rebounder, it may decide that the 1–3–1 zone is the best defense to use. Defensively, a 1–3–1 zone has definite advantages. It is strong under the basket and on the sides, although weak on the corners. However, the corners can be covered by the following maneuvers shown in Diagram 82.

Weakness of zone lies in corners and outside. Another weakness lies outside. Since only one defensive player covers two men, the latter can maneuver themselves for a set shot. Therefore, the front man on the 1–3–1 zone must be exceptionally fast, for he is in essence a chaser.

1-3-1 is a good offensive zone. Offensively, the 1–3–1 is better than the 2–3. It can get four men down court relatively fast, although not as fast as the 2–1–2 or 3–2. Since the forwards can hit the sidelines without trouble, and the middle lane is taken care of by two men, the 1–3–1 is a good fast breaking zone.

PRESS DEFENSE

Many basketball teams that fast break choose a press because it is easier to break from this defense. Through a full court press, many more breaking opportunities arise from interceptions and bad passes.

There are two types of press. There are two types of presses. One arises from a man-to-man; the other from a zone. In setting up a full court press, it is important to pick up the opponents in the back court and keep up the pressure all the way down court. The three areas should be clearly covered before the original pass out. See Diagram 83.

In a man-to-man press, after the initial pass out, the players must "dog" their opponents as the ball is brought down the court.

Zone press differs from man-to-man press. The zone press differs from the man-to-man press by having the players retreat into the forecourt guarding certain areas. Although they line up as in the man-to-man press, covering the three lanes, they remain in these lanes, moving into the back court as Diagram 84 shows.

Press offers more breaking opportunities. The press offers more fast breaking opportunities, since the offense is forced into more errors. A good press team will have definite patterns the moment an opponent makes an error. The press will force the opponent

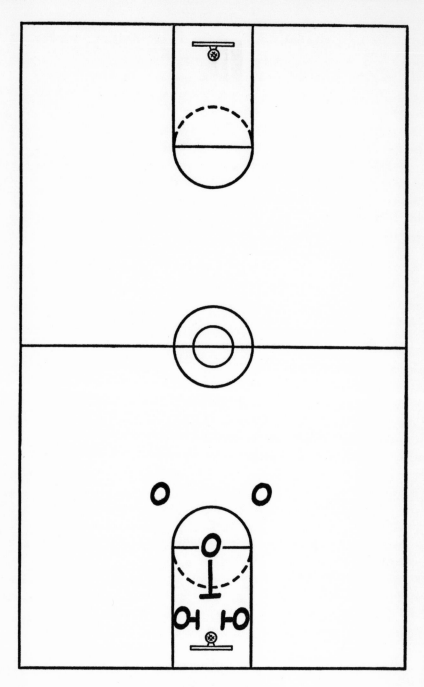

Diagram 77.

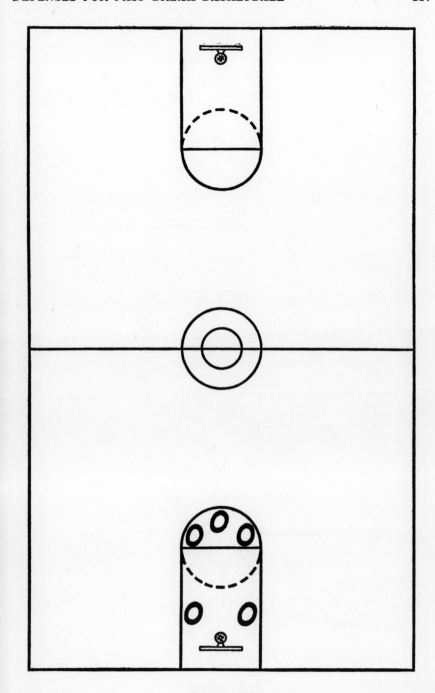

Diagram 78.

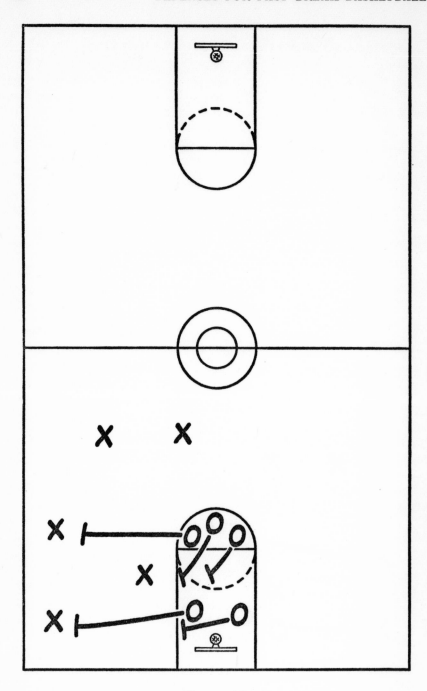

Diagram 79.

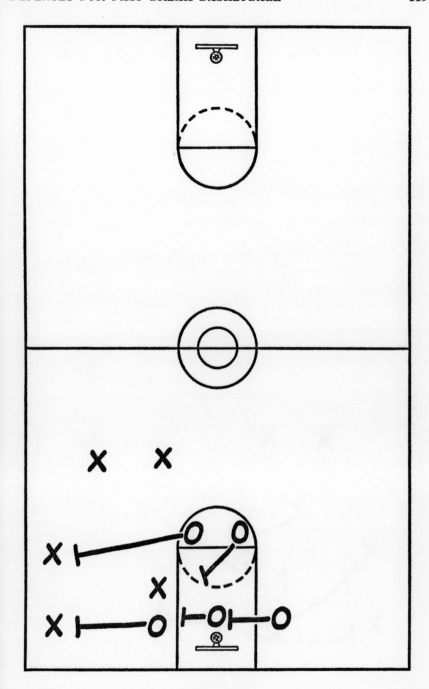

Diagram 80.

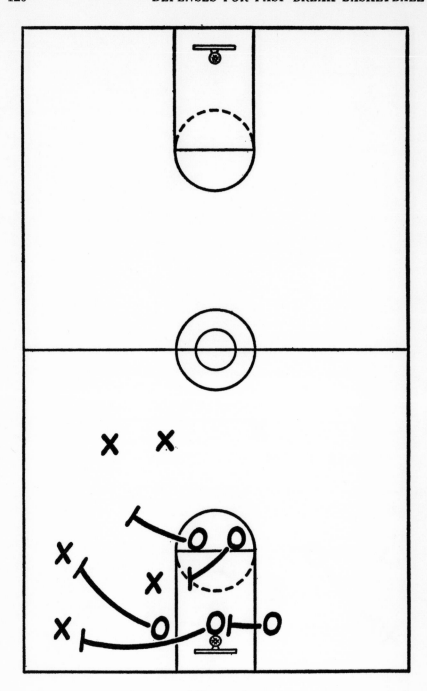

Diagram 81.

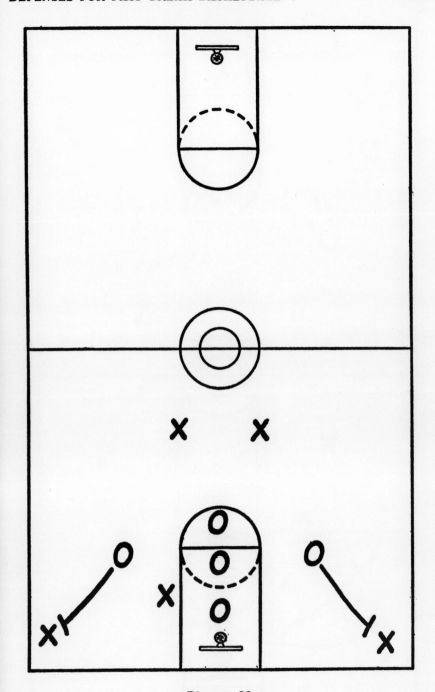

Diagram 82.

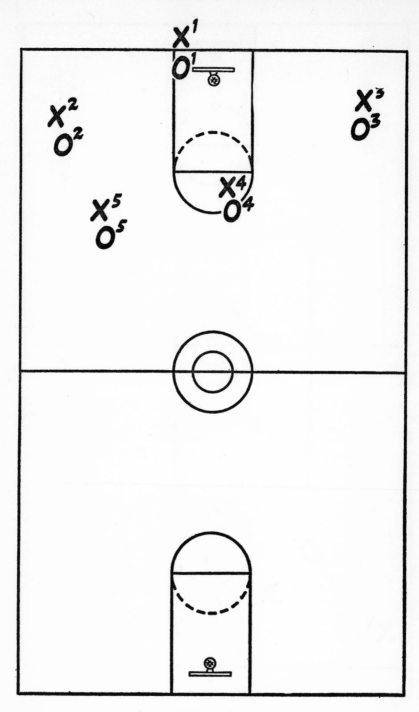

Diagram 83.

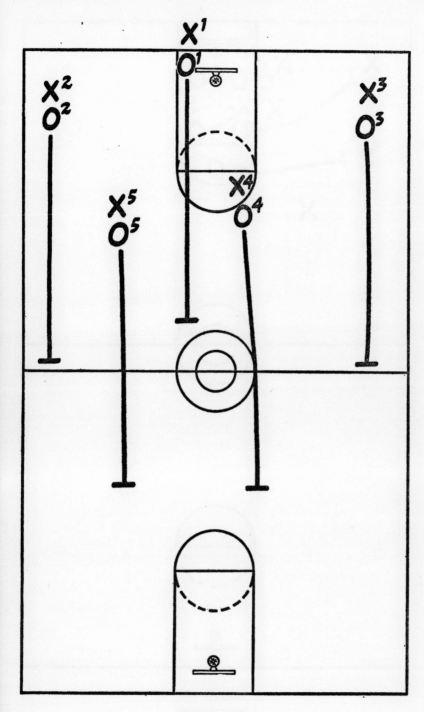

Diagram 84.

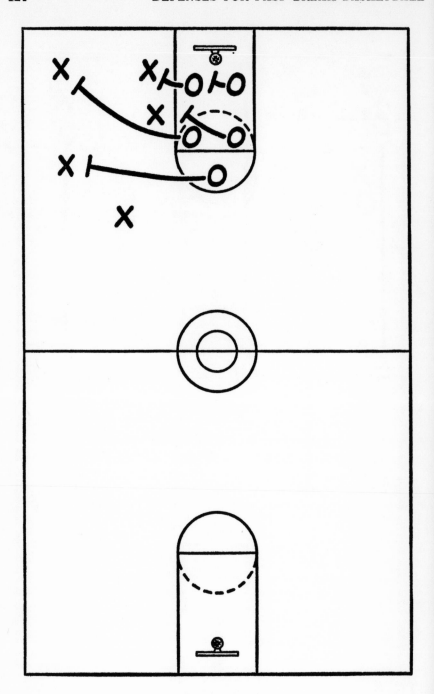

Diagram 85.

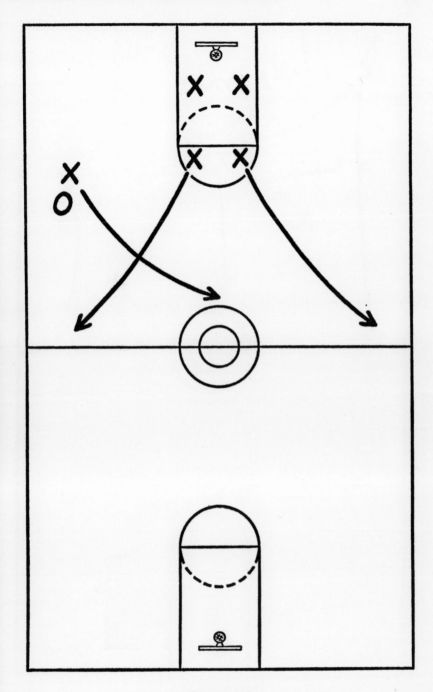

Diagram 86.

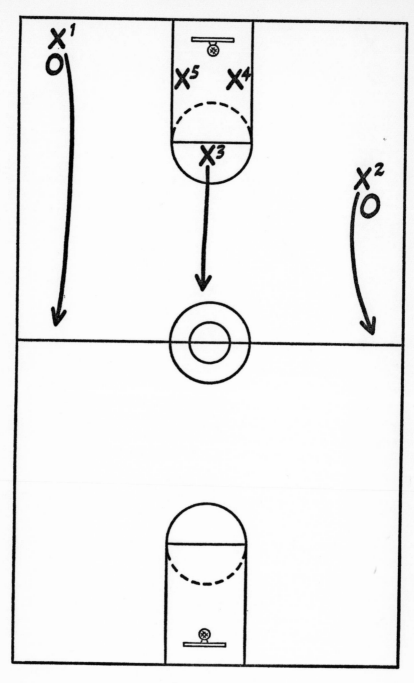

Diagram 87.

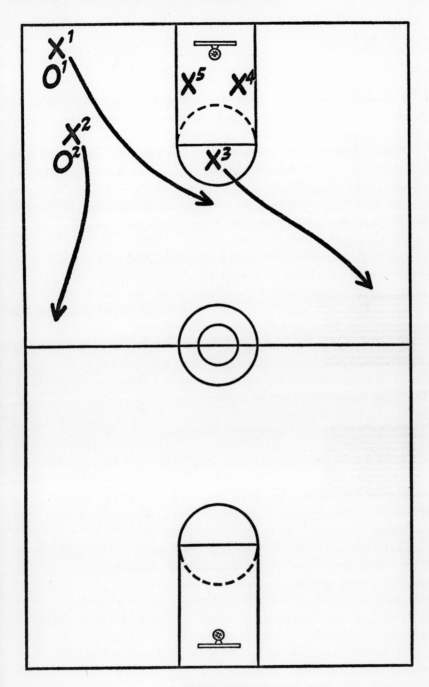

Diagram 88.

to hurry its shots, so that breaking from rebounding will prevail throughout the game.

MAN-TO-MAN ZONE DEFENSE

A combination defense that the writer has used effectively for fast break purposes takes the best features of the man-to-man defense and incorporates them into a zone pattern.

Middle lane is kept closed. The two forwards line up as they would in the 1–2–2. However, they follow their opponents into the corners. They play their opponents outside and inside. The two guards play their inside opponents as in the man-to-man. However, they do not follow them when they leave the inside lanes. The middle lane is always kept closed. The front man covers the outside man and will go with him if he cuts into the middle lane. On the sides the maneuvers are as shown in Diagram 85.

The right forward covers the corner man. The front man covers the side. The right guard covers the man under the basket. The left forward drops into the slot inside the foul line.

This is a good breaking defense. This man-to-man zone is strong offensively because the three front men are ready for breaking. The forwards playing the same area will break to the sidelines. The front man goes down the middle.

MULTIPLE DEFENSE

Football men have adopted a multiple defense by combining the best features of various defenses. The same principle is being adopted in basketball. By using several defenses, you prevent your opponents from using set patterns. Their offense is thrown into confusion.

This defense is used to stop great scorers. The multiple defense is best used when adjusted to meet opponent personnel. If the opponents have one great scorer and four mediocre players, a four man zone with one player playing man-to-man will best stop your opponents. Since the great scorer will be "dogged" everywhere, he will have few good shots. If he succeeds in breaking away from his guard, he will be picked up by one of the four men in the zone. With such pressure on him, the great scorer's potential will be greatly decreased. The four-man zone will take care of the other players.

Fast breaking from this defense is set up by having the two front men on the 2–2 zone break to the sidelines. The man-to-man player breaks down the middle. See Diagram 86.

If a team has two great scorers and three mediocre players, it is best to assign your two best guards to cover the "stars" and use a 1–2 zone to cover the other players. You will be playing percentage as you invite the poorer scorers to shoot while bottling up the better players.

Fast breaking from this defense is more difficult as the two man-to-man players will be out of position. They should drive down the sideline nearest to them when they get the ball. The front man in the 1–2 zone will go down the middle lane. If they find themselves in this position as shown in Diagram 87, they can fast break.

A difficulty arises when both man-to-man guards are on the same side. They can overcome this by shouting to the middle man to take the other side. Diagram 88 shows how they will break.

This pattern is difficult and will require much practice, especially in shouting advice to X^3 to take the side. Nevertheless, sometimes offense must be sacrificed for defensive strength.

Use the press in the backcourt. A good defense to use against a poor ball handling team is to press in the backcourt. If the opponent has one good dribbler, it is best to cover him so close as to prevent his getting the ball. This maneuver will force the poorer ball handlers to bring the ball down court.

If your opponents like to cut down the middle, a zone will stop them.

If your opponents cannot hit from the outside, a 2–3 zone is best.

If your opponents hit well from the outside, a 3–2 or a combination man-to-man zone will work to advantage.

If your opponents rebound well, a combination man-to-man zone will hamper them.

If your opponents have five excellent shots, a man-to-man will minimize their strength.

Most coaches are acquainted with the different types of zone and man-to-man defenses. However, there are two defenses the writer wishes you to consider. One is the combination man-to-man zone.

In a junior varsity game between Canastota, New York, High School and Vernon-Verona-Sherill, the latter had a team consisting of three very tall boys and two medium sized ones; Canastota had a small team. To offset the superiority in size, Canastota used a combination defense and so confused its opponent that the latter repeatedly threw passes into the hands of the two goal tenders. What should have been an easy game for V.V.S. turned into a rout for Canastota.

During the 1957 season, Canastota's varsity, finding itself weak offensively, decided to use a multiple defense to confound its opponents. Playing against Camden High School, Canastota used a 3 man zone and the other two played man-to-man. Camden had two of the best scorers in the Tri-Valley League. Its other players were mediocre. Canastota assigned its two best guards to cover the Camden stars; it set up a 1–2 zone for its other players.

Being accustomed to feeding these two stars, Camden followed the same pattern in this game. The two stars were so "dogged" throughout the game that their shots were often hurried, with the result they were held to a combined total of twelve points. The poorer players, being forced to shoot, hit a low percentage of shots. Camden was discouraged by this defense and Canastota scored one of the biggest upsets of the season.

In another important league game, upon which the championship depended, Canastota scored another upset because it used a multiple defense. V.V.S. had a very tall varsity team, with two boys about 6'5". V.V.S. had used its height to defeat every league opponent. In this game Canastota began with a 2–3 zone. It did well for a quarter. The moment that V.V.S. showed signs of penetrating Canastota's defense, the latter shifted to a press. As soon as the boys showed signs of fatigue, they turned to a 2–1–2.

In the second half Canastota changed to a man-to-man zone. This constant shifting of defense so confused V.V.S. that it was unable to utilize its great height. Being behind by ten points in the last quarter, V.V.S. went into a press. For a few minutes it confused Canastota, but the latter was well schooled on fast break principles, especially the ones on breaking against a press. Leaving itself wide open, V.V.S. could not cope with this strategic move and Canastota scored very vital quick break baskets which decided the game. The multiple defense had enabled Canastota to give V.V.S. its first defeat.

10

SUCCESSFUL FAST BREAK COURT STRATEGY

OUTSTANDING COACHES ARE USUALLY SOUND COURT STRATEGISTS. The fast break coach must be a good strategist because he must prepare his attack to meet the defensive switches of his opponents. Failure to do so will mean defeats in close games. For example, if the opponents are clogging the middle defensively on the break, the offense should concentrate on bringing the ball down the sides. If the defense concentrates on covering the right side and center, the left forward should drive down court.

In an important scholastic game, the defensive strategy was to cover the opponent's center and right forward in the back court the moment that they took the ball out. These two were the backbone of the fast break offense. By this strategy, the left forward was left open.

Diagram 89 shows the defensive alignment.

Instead of taking advantage of this opening, the coach of the fast break team became too excited to notice this maneuver, with the result his two stars continued to take the ball down court and were tied up. They lost the game by one point when they should have won it easily.

Poor strategy lost game. Poor court strategy on the part of this coach cost him the game. His opponent had planned a strategic game, bottling up the opponent's star players. A good strategist would have counteracted this strategy with the move mentioned above—feeding the left forward instead of the right forward or center.

131

Coach's knowledge will determine strategy. Court strategy is dependent upon the coach's knowledge of the game, upon his knowledge of different modes of attack and of defense, and upon his ability to observe the specific skills and weaknesses of the opponent's players. When he has such talent, he can make the right change in his attack or defense, confusing his opponents so that he can offset the superior ability of the opponent's personnel. Underdog teams score upsets because of sound court strategy.

STRATEGY PLANNED BEFOREHAND

The coach must prepare himself for any exigency before he plays. He should know beforehand what to do if the opponent plays him in the back court, if he presses, if he double-teams his superior players.

No strategy necessary when opponents play orthodox ball. When your opponents do not trouble to hamper your rebounder or do not pick up your players in the back court, you need not worry about the ultimate success of your attack. But when they do either, your team should be prepared. You should know every move your opponent may make to slow you down.

If your opponents crowd your rebounder, instruct this player to dribble off to the sideline before making his pass out. See Diagram 90.

This move will enable him to clear himself of his opponents. It will also foil the defensive strategy of your opponents.

If your opponents press in the back court, the maneuvers shown in Diagram 91 will enable you to fast break.

X^1 throws X^2 who comes in fast to receive the pass. X^2 immediately throws to X^1. The latter throws to X^4 who has broken from his man and gone to the sideline. X^3 breaks down the middle area. X^5 goes down the left sideline, and X^4 goes down the right sideline. Thus, the offense has broken away from the press for a quick break.

Lack of planning leads to defeats. If the coach is not well prepared for this maneuver, he may be defeated. Sound strategy requires him to be well prepared before the game, so that he can call time out and have his team exploit the opponent's defense.

Switch offense to confuse opponents. An opponent may double-team your star player. If he does so, he will leave your weaker player open. If you have prepared well, you will exploit

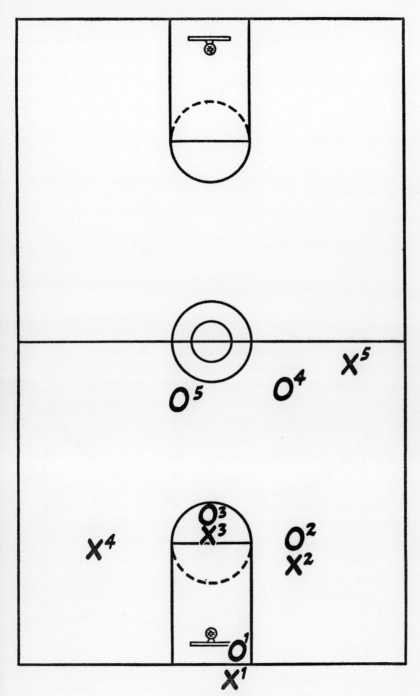

Diagram 89.

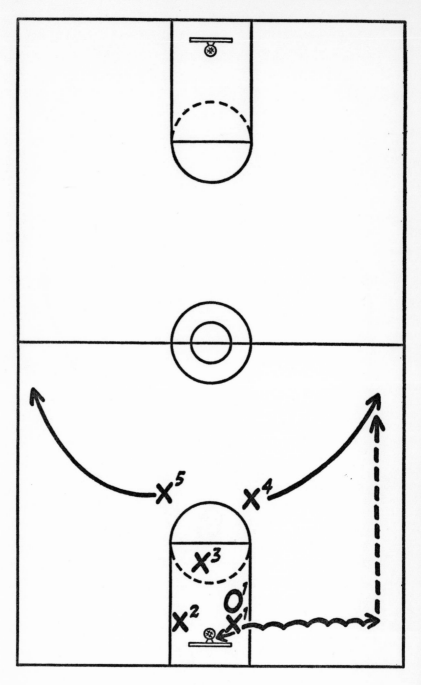

Diagram 90.

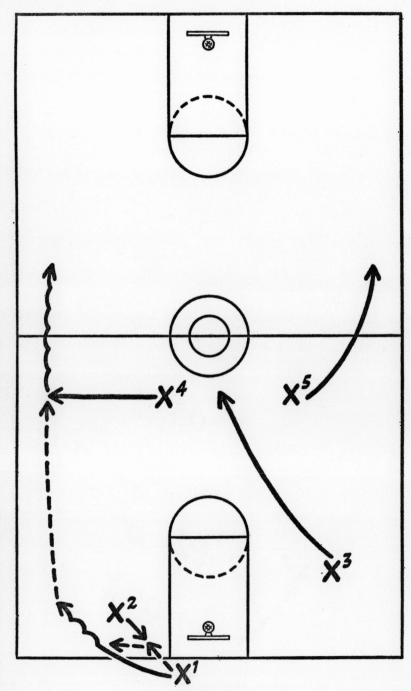

Diagram 91.

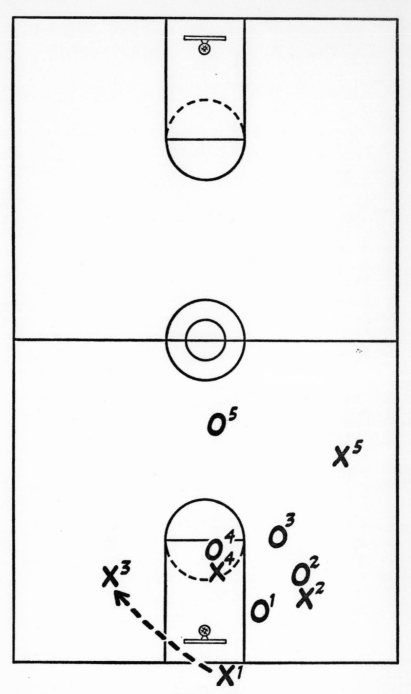

Diagram 92.

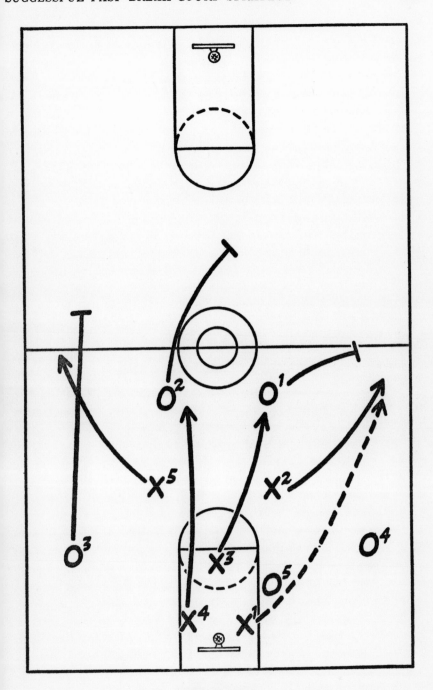

Diagram 93.

this move by a simple switch. Instead of having your star player handle the ball as he does customarily, have him act as decoy, keeping the two men on him and liberating his team mates to drive in. The moment that one of the defensive players leaves the star player to cover the other weaker player, you can have your star swing back to his customary role. See Diagram 92.

X^2 who ordinarily receives the pass from X^1 on the out-of-bounds will not handle the ball as long as O^1 and O^2 cover him. X^3 will receive the pass. But when O^1 and O^2 swing over to cover X^3 and X^4, X^2 can drive in as he does usually.

No team can afford to keep more than two men back on offense without hurting its attack. When the opponent is well prepared and sends three men back on defense the moment it loses the ball, that poses a serious problem for the coach. To offset this move, you can prepare for this eventuality. Diagram 93 shows how to overcome this strategy.

X^1 throws to X^2 who is covered by O^1. X^2 throws to X^3 who is covered by O^2. X^3 passes to X^4. If O^3 covers X^4, the latter passes to X^5. By getting 4 on 3, the fast break is maintained.

STRATEGY DURING THE GAME

The good coach uses strategy during the game by preparing well beforehand. If he knows that his opponent has certain weaknesses in personnel, he should work his plays through these players.

Play opponents' weaknesses. Every team has certain strong points. You should not work through these strengths. If a team has strong rebounders, the offensive patterns should eliminate chance shots and take those which have a high percentage of scoring. If a team shows strength in front of the basket, drive in on the sides. If a team uses a zone and has strong rebounders on the right side, shoot from that side so that the rebounding is against their strength.

Against a zone team using a 2–3 zone, shoot from the sides. Against a strong zone team, the strategy should be to tire the defense by passing and passing until the opponents are out of position.

The over-all strategy of the fast-break team is to wear out the opposition during the first three quarters in order to crush them in the last quarter. To accomplish this, you should fast break throughout the game. You should not become discouraged if you do not break away consistently during the early stages of the game since the opponents are still strong. Constant pressure will eventually wear them down.

Change defense during game. Good strategy demands changes throughout the game on defense to "throw off" the offense. By using different zones or combination zone and man-to-man, your offense will confuse the offense and cause it to operate below peak efficiency. The defense you select will naturally depend on your personnel and that of your opponent.

TIME OUTS

Few coaches use time-outs judiciously. Every time out taken should have a reason. Try to take about two time outs during the first half and retain at least two for the closing moments of the game when you must resort to game-winning or game-saving devices. Of course, this is subject to the changes the game may demand. For example, if you are encountering difficulties either on offense or defense during the early minutes of the game, it is better to take the necessary time-outs to straighten out these difficulties than to allow the game to be lost in the first half. The time-outs left for the close of the game will be meaningless then.

When should a time-out be taken? Do not take it for one player. A substitution can straighten out his trouble. It should be taken for the entire team. If your players cannot fathom an opponent's defense, take time out to explain how to pierce this defense. If your defense is being riddled, take time out to explain where the flaw lies.

Take time out to cool a hot team. Take time out to cool a hot team or to inspire a cold one. Take care not to take time out to berate the players. That will not help. Explanations should be given as to the causes of failure. Encouragement rather than censure will be more helpful.

Take time out to make switches in defense. Take time to arrange for a change of defense or switch in offense to meet the changing offensive and defensive maneuvers of your opponent. If your opponents have been using a zone and suddenly switch to man-to-man, take time to prepare your players for new assignments. Some coaches have success in meeting these switches by preparing their players during the week, but most players are easily confused by these switches. The writer saw a good Connecticut team in the 1958 National Collegiate tournament go to pieces when Dartmouth, its opponent, switched from a man-to-man to zone. Connecticut kept on trying to feed its pivot as it had been doing and had some 20 passes intercepted.

Most important time outs are those of closing minutes. Undoubtedly the most important time outs are those taken in the closing minutes of the game. If you are behind five points or more at the four minute mark, order a press defense. To make sure every player presses, take time out to explain assignments. Players under the emotional stress of the game forget to carry out assignments. One player who fails to do so ruins the team effort. There will be no excuse for miscarriage of individual responsibility when you explain it at the time out.

Do not take chances if you are ahead. If you are ahead by a few points with a few minutes to go, it is foolish to take chances. It is much wiser to play safe. Even professional teams have lost games they seemingly had won by not playing safe in the closing minutes. No well-schooled team should lose a game in which it is leading by 3 or 4 points in the closing minutes. Its strategy should be to force the opponents to commit themselves, leaving an opening, and then to take advantage of this opening.

Hold on to ball if ahead. By playing a little further out from the basket and retaining the ball through a series of pre-arranged patterns of passes, a team forces its opponents to come out and try to take the ball away. As they do so, in their anxiety to get the ball, they will make mistakes. If they fail to make them, the offense will continue to pass. As long as the offense retains the ball, it cannot lose. The defense becomes more and more anxious and eventually will make a mistake. That is when the game should be salted away.

CLOSING MINUTE

Be careful in last minute if ahead. The strategy of the last minute should be a careful one. If you are ahead by a point or two, the strategy is to retain the ball and look for layups only. If you are a point or two behind, the strategy is to get a running screen for a layup.

The strategy when the score is tied is not to take a shot until it is certain. Too many teams will gamble all on a set shot. The percentage is against this. The better strategy is to pass until the last five seconds. Then a player should drive in around a momentary screen. Under such circumstances, the defense will either allow him to drive, with the ensuing shot possibly winning the game, or it will foul him. In either case, the percentage is greatly in favor of the offensive player.

Two actual examples, one of lack of closing minute strategy and one of its proper use, will emphasize the points made above.

In the state tournament finals at Boston Garden in 1949, Barnstable High School was playing a strong opponent. Using a controlled fast break, Barnstable gained a six point lead with three minutes to go. A well-schooled team would have won this game by applying the principles given above. However, Barnstable failed to use them. Instead of using a freezing offense, forcing the opponents to come to them and taking advantage of openings, Barnstable tightened up and allowed their opponents to score two baskets.

With a minute to go and a two-point lead, the strategy was for Barnstable to call time and prepare its moves. Barnstable, however, did not do so and went right on with the wrong strategy. Its opponent tied the score with 15 seconds to go. A team that was well schooled in the closing minute strategy could still have won the game, but Barnstable, in its anxiety, threw the ball away. An opposing player took a desperate 30 foot shot at the whistle. He missed, but an excited Barnstable player struck him after the shot. The opposing player made the foul, winning the game and the championship for his school.

Poor closing-minutes and last-minute strategy caused the Barnstable coach to lose a game which he should have won. He lost a championship because he lacked this knowledge.

The following year, in a Cape Cod league game, this same Barnstable team was leading its rival, Bourne High School, by twelve points with six minutes to go. However, the fast break had tired a tense Barnstable team so that it lost nine of these points in the next three minutes. Having learned his lesson the previous year, the Barnstable coach had time called. He explained to his players that the game was won if they relaxed and followed instructions. He mapped out to them how to play the freezing offense which they had practiced all year.

The hot Bourne team continued to play aggressively, taking chances. Since Barnstable kept the ball away, Bourne kept right after them, leaving many openings. Barnstable methodically took advantage of these openings, scoring twelve points to their opponent's none in the remaining three minutes, and eventually winning by 15 points.

These examples show the importance of court strategy in determining close games.

11

DEFENSIVE STRATEGY AGAINST FAST BREAK TEAMS

As POTENT AS THE FAST BREAK HAS BECOME, IT CAN BE SLOWED down. There are various ways of accomplishing this. The most common methods are pressing in the back court, keeping two men back, pressing the rebounding men, and slowing down the attack.

Tall man prevents pass out. Fire-horse teams depend on getting the ball out-of-bounds rapidly to catch the defense off guard. The best way to slow down this attack is to have your tallest man play in front of the player taking the ball out-of-bounds. By having your player keep his hands up, you will force the offensive man to slow his pass out, since he cannot throw over your player's hands.

Some years ago, in the 1945 N.I.T. tournament to be exact, the greatest fire-horse basketball team in the country, Rhode Island, had stormed from a 21-point first half deficit into a 4 point advantage in the first ten minutes of the second half. During these ten minutes of the second half, Rhode Island, by pressing more closely, so upset St. Johns that the latter threw away many passes or had them intercepted. Rhode Island was also breaking the moment it took the ball out-of-bounds and catching St. Johns off guard. A 42-21 St. Johns half-time lead was dissipated and Rhode Island led 55-51.

At this stage, Joe Lapchick, St. Johns' coach, one of the greatest court strategists in the game, had Ivy Summers, his center, stand in front of the rapidly tiring Rhode Island guard as soon as he obtained possession of the ball. This move prevented the guard from getting the ball away to set up the fast break. Rhode Island was slowed down to such an extent that it was able to score only 5 points the last

142

ten minutes of the game in contrast to the 34 it had scored the first ten minutes of the second half. Through this slowing down maneuver, St. Johns not only stopped the firehorse tactics of Rhode Island but it also broke down their morale.

PRESS IN THE BACK COURT

Back court press leads to stolen passes. Against a good fast break team, it may be best for you to press them in the back court. By pressing, you may steal misdirected passes. A team that finds its offensive passes stolen may become discouraged, if not completely demoralized. The back court press should not be used as a slowing down process if your opponents have definite patterns against such a defense. If they do have such patterns, your defense may boomerang.

Some teams have found a zone press a good back court defense against a breaking team. They usually set it up in this fashion. See Diagram 94.

Defense attempts to intercept passes. The defense plays the ball and attempts to steal passes. They not only slow down the initial pass out but also try to intercept it. If the initial pass out is successfully made, the defense fights the offense all the way down court, keeping the three lanes covered. In other words, the 2–1–2 zone defense merely retreats until it is in its own defensive territory.

A slight deviation from the zone press usually thrown against the break in the back court is shown in Diagram 95.

Pass out is difficult. This pattern is better because it makes the initial pass out difficult, and yet covers the sides well for possible interceptions. When the initial pass is made successfully, O^1 retreats into the center area, fighting the opposition all the way down court.

TWO MEN BACK

Two men back slows up break. Another method of slowing down a fast break is to keep two men back on defense at all times. These two should retreat in a definite manner when the offense comes down court. The best way to slow down the offense and enable more defensive men to get back into defensive territory is given in the following: Diagram 96 shows the manner of retreat.

O^1 and O^2 retreat cautiously without getting over to cover the fast break forwards on the sidelines. The temptation will be great to

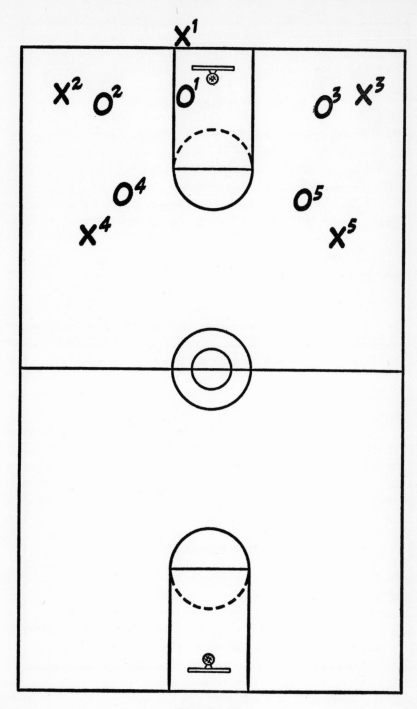

Diagram 94.

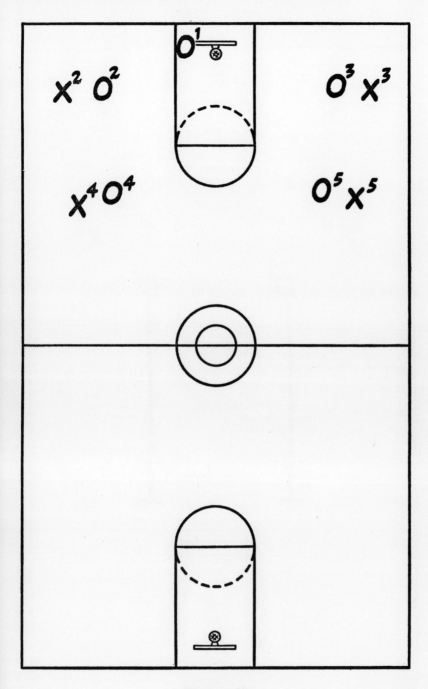

Diagram 95.

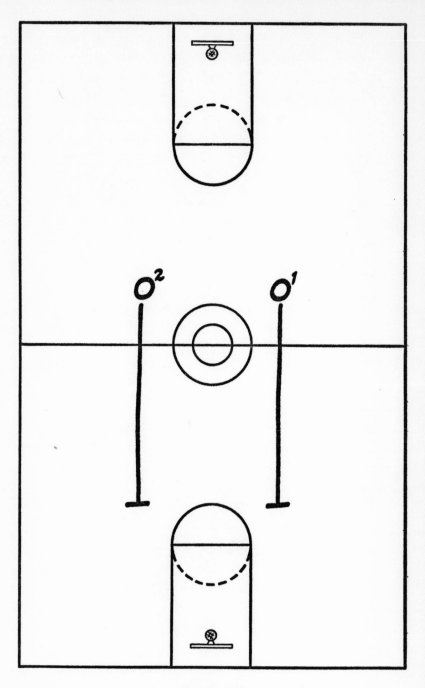

Diagram 96.

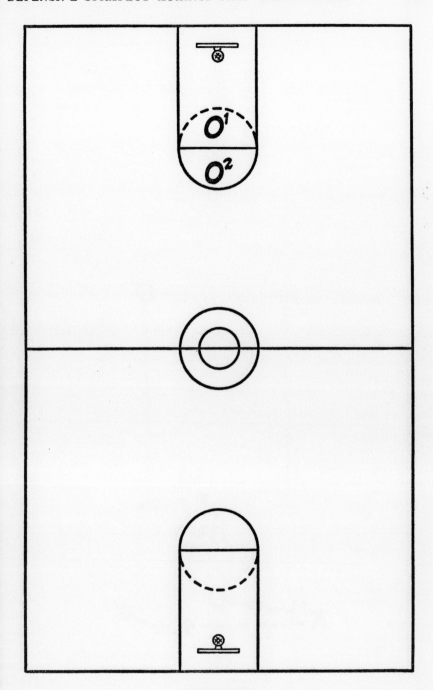

Diagram 97.

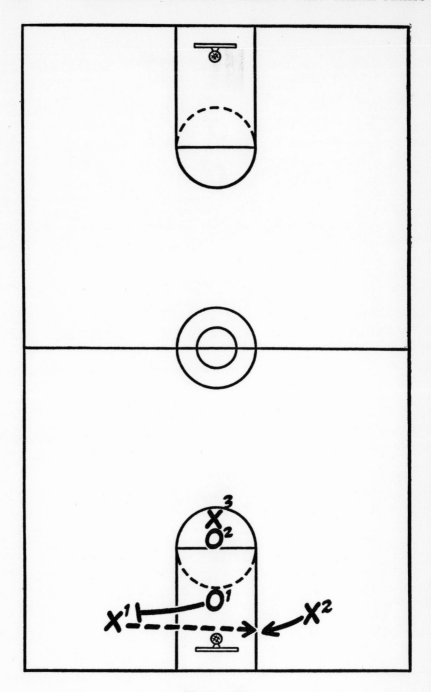

Diagram 98.

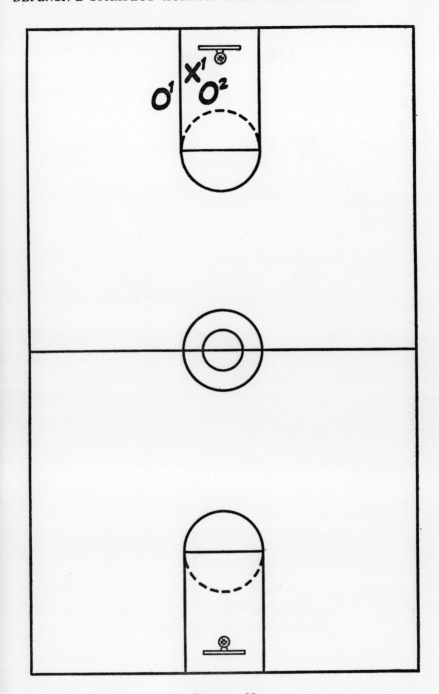

Diagram 99.

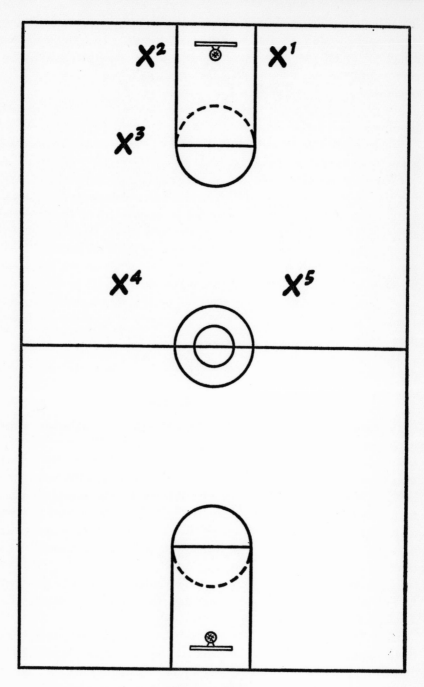

Diagram 100.

leave the middle lane in order to cover a forward who is dribbling down to the sideline. But to do so is suicide. The moment that either O^1 or O^2 cover the sideline, they leave two areas open—the center and the other side—with but one man to play them. It is obvious that this will lead to layup baskets. By remaining in the above positions, O^1 and O^2 can cover three lanes fairly well and still be in position to rebound.

Some teams like to use the following two men as shown in Diagram 97 to slow down the break.

Clogging middle lane to stop break. The writer has never felt this defense to be too good because any outstanding fast break team will outmaneuver the defense for an easy layup on the opposite side. This defense is set up to break the back of the three-lane break by clogging the middle. However, it weakens itself on both sides. A good breaking club will vary its attack and strike on the sides. A forward will drive all the way down the side. If O^1 or O^2 do not come over, they will continue to drive until they reach the basket. Then O^1 must come over to cover. The moment he does, a bounce pass to the other side leads to an easy layup. See Diagram 98.

This defense is very effective if your opponent's fast break is predicated on a middle lane offensive.

PRESS REBOUND MAN

Pressing rebound man slows break. Another method of slowing down the break is to crowd the rebounders. By crowding the rebounder, the defense makes it difficult for him to make the initial pass to start the break. This maneuver may cause too-frequent fouling, but it will prevent breaking after rebounds. The defensive team may find that the crowded rebounder will hurry his passes so that many interceptions may be made. This calculated maneuver will not only reduce quick break baskets but will also demoralize the offense.

If the defense finds that the rebounder is too clever to be crowded by one man, the following defense may accomplish the same thing as Diagram 99 illustrates.

Have O^1 and O^2 forget about getting back on defense and focus their attention on the rebounder. O^1 crowds X^1 on one side and O^2 crowds him on the other side. By keeping their hands up, they make it difficult for X^1 to get that pass out. After they have accomplished this, they can get back on defense.

SLOW DOWN THE ATTACK

Deliberate attack slows down break. Another method of slowing down the break is to have a deliberate attack. By playing possession ball and not taking poor shots, a team can keep the ball away from the fast break team. It is a known fact that breaking teams become impatient when they cannot obtain possession of the ball. A team that uses a very deliberate attack will find that its opponent will be rushing its attack when it does get the ball, with the result that it will make many errors. Poor hurried shots and interceptions will often result.

The deliberate attack should be planned to force a breaking team to move a great deal in its effort to cover the offense. A slow, set, deliberate attack will also plan its defense well, so that it gets back after it loses the ball. In the finals of the New Jersey State Tournament between Weehawken High School, one of the fastest high school teams in the country, and Merchantville High, the latter's coach was able to score one of the greatest upsets in the state's history through his very carefully planned offensive and defensive strategy.

Weehawken, which had been scoring as much as 99 points against top-notch opposition, which had won the state title the year before, and which had defeated the best teams in the state, was a great favorite to win because of its tremendous breaking attack and its great array of sharpshooters. Yet the Merchantville coach had scouted them so well that he knew he would have to drop his two guards completely out of the play. In bringing the ball into play, his offensive alignment was as shown in Diagram 100.

From this position the Merchantville guards, X^4 and X^5, were always in position to stop the Weehawken forwards. However, the Merchantville 6'4" center, being an important "cog" on the offense, was stationed under the basket. It is obvious that he was out of position to pick up the Weehawken center, so the Merchantville coach had X^3, who was stationed near the foul line, drop into the middle lane the moment his team lost the ball.

This move enabled Merchantville's scoring aces, the forward and the center, to devote themselves to offense. Since they were tall, they were able to follow every rebound until they either scored or tied up the guards. Weehawken's fast break was slowed down because the Merchantville team worked the ball deliberately to these two men. When they could not shoot, they passed out again to the guards who would pass in to these two until an opening occurred. They kept this up until good shots resulted. Since the two men inside were excellent shots, they almost invariably scored. Meanwhile, the two guards remained stationary, ever ready to cover the Weehawken forwards.

With this deliberate attack and defense, Merchantville forced Weehawken to play a slow game. The result was a great upset.

The various defenses described will slow down any fast break team. If all these defenses are used, you will find that no breaking team can score at will against you with easy layups.

12

HOW TO SCOUT
A FAST BREAK TEAM

Wʜᴀᴛ ᴀʀᴇ ᴛʜᴇ ᴛʜɪɴɢs ᴛᴏ ʟᴏᴏᴋ ꜰᴏʀ ɪɴ sᴄᴏᴜᴛɪɴɢ ᴀ ꜰᴀsᴛ ʙʀᴇᴀᴋ team? Your report should cover opponent personnel and style of break used. It should be complete enough to enable you to plan a defense.

Size, speed, and shooting skill. In scouting the personnel of your opponents, notice the size of the players, how well they use their size, their over-all speed, their shooting skill, areas they prefer in shooting, who does the shooting, and percentage of shots made.

In scouting the style of fast break used, observe the specific defense used, how well it is used, and its weaknesses.

SIZE OF PLAYERS

In the modern game height plays a great part. Since rebounds usually initiate the break, the size of the boys who rebound is of great importance. We should know where the tall boys are used in the break. We may notice that the tall boys are weak in dribbling. This information is invaluable to us since we can place our best guards on these boys to tie them up and hamper their fast break.

If we see that the tall boys are used near the basket, we may counteract this by placing fast men on them so that they can break away from them on offense. Knowledge of this may cause these taller boys to be wary on offense, for fear of having their men break away from them.

Get inside of big boys. If we notice that the tall boys are used in certain areas for offensive rebounding, we can counteract this

154

strategy by setting up a defense to get inside position on these players.

Most big men have definite areas they like to play on defense. Knowledge of this may be helpful as we can plan to get inside position and counteract their size.

Use a swarming defense on big boys. What these big men do with the rebound when they get it is very important, because the pass out initiates the break. Observing that the player passes as soon as he captures the rebound, we may decide to play a swarming defense to delay this initial pass, thus hampering the break.

SPEED

Since the fast break is dependent on speed, we should know the relative speed of our opponents. The faster the personnel, the more difficult will it be to stop their break. If we see that the overall speed of our opponents is very good, we may suggest in our report to use a very deliberate game to slow down their attack.

Most fast break teams have one or two exceptionally fast men and others of moderate speed. This fact is important to know as we can place our fast men on these boys. We must also adjust our defense to meet the exceptional speed of these players. We may decide to play our defensive guards a few yards further back on offense and thus minimize the jump that these fast players may get on our defense.

Notice the area of the break. In scouting speed, notice the area of the break. If the exceptionally fast boys break, let us say, on the right side and in the center, we can direct our guards to drop back in these areas the moment we lost the ball.

Observe where these fast boys play defensively so that we can direct our offense away from them.

SHOOTING

No phase of the fast break is of more importance to us than the shooting skill of our opponents, since that may defeat us. A quick break team differs from other teams in shooting as it depends more on layups and on fast shooting. Most players have varying degrees of skill on layup shots. Seeing that the right forward has an exceptional layup shot, we can use this information to set up our defense.

We may decide to play this player closer on the break, forcing the other two to take the layups.

By playing percentage we may save many valuable baskets. If we notice that the right and left forwards are exceptionally accurate on the layups and the center is weak, we will instruct our defensive guards to watch the forwards closer on the defensive retreat and force the center to take the shots. This maneuver may well save the game for you.

Missed layups lead to loss of game. In a state tournament game, one team used a three lane break. On five occasions the three-lane break was on, and four times the middle man missed his layup. Eventually this was the difference in the game. By sloughing off him, the defensive guards forced the poorer shot to make the try, and he missed four important attempts.

Notice sharp shooters. When the breaking team takes hurried shots the moment it has anyone open, we should see which players are sharp on this attack. A chart taken of shots taken by each player will be invaluable to us as we can plan our defense accordingly.

DEFENSE USED

Against 2-3 shoot from side. The zone is used by most fast break teams to set up its break. The type used will be of much help to us. Observing that a 2–3 is used, we can plan our offense so that we can get our key men on the side for set shots. We can also instruct these side men to drop back immediately on defense in order to cover the three lanes defensively.

If our opponents use a 2–1–2, we can plan a 1–2–2 offense, with our two big men near the basket and our two best shots on the sides to riddle the defense. This offense will also enable us to get three men back immediately to cover the three lanes to break up their attack.

Shoot from corners against 3-2. If our opponents use a 3–2, we can plan to use a 2–1–2 offense. By keeping our best shots in the corners and our big man near the basket, we will be playing our opponents' weakness. We will also be keeping two men back to hamper their fast break. This defense is the most difficult to play because if we make errors on offense our opponents will capitalize on them, since they will be in excellent position to break.

Shoot from corners against 1-3-1. If we observe a 1–3–1 defense, we can plan a 1–2–2 offense, getting our best shots in the corners and our best rebounders near the basket. This offense is weak on defense but is strong on offense. The gamble is to score sufficiently and thus offer our opponents less chances to break. Since the defense is farther back, it must go farther on offense, giving the corner men a chance to get back on defense.

The scouting report should show the personnel weaknesses of these various zones, so that the offense can plan to work its plays through these areas.

Notice who breaks to the sideline in man-to-man. If our opponents use a man-to-man defense for their break, we should see which players break to the sidelines and how well they do it. Notice who goes down the all-important middle lane. Do our opponents break into this lane? If they do not, we can plan on having two fast guards cover their forwards. We should observe who initiates the break. How do they set it up? Knowledge of this will help us set up our defensive strategy.

The fast break is a potent offense, but no offense works at maximum efficiency when its opponent knows how to play against it. Good scouting may be worth 20 points or more to a team, often enough to enable it to defeat a superior opponent.

We shall give the following example to illustrate how scouting enabled a team to score a great upset against an outstanding fast breaking team.

North Arlington, New Jersey, High School had won forty straight games, gaining the state title in 1956-57. It had swept everything before it during the 1957-58 season, reaching the finals of the Bergen County tournament. Its opponent, Hackensack, after a mediocre season, had reached its peak in the tournament.

North Arlington was the favorite to win. However, Hackensack had scouted its opponent very well, learning that the former used a fire-horse style of ball. Knowing that North Arlington threw long passes to start its break, Hackensack decided to have its big men prevent the initial pass, and have its players drop back immediately on defense. The result was that North Arlington could not get its passes off to start its break.

Another strategy was to play North Arlington's great scorers very closely, forcing them to hurry their shots or have other players do the shooting. Being forced to play Hackensack's game, North Arlington's offense was stymied. Its forty game streak came to an abrupt close.

13

TIPS ON HOW TO INSTALL
THE FAST BREAK

W HEN YOU DECIDE TO INSTALL THE FAST BREAK, YOU MAY BE faced with many troublesome problems. If you are a beginning coach, your first difficult problem is to convince your players that your style will eventually bring successful results. You must, however, caution your players that it will take time to accomplish this, since the fast break requires exact timing which comes only after much practice and experience. When the boys become discouraged, as they will at times, you must be patient with them and confident that results will come inevitably. The quick break may take longer in being installed as an offense, but the results warrant this extra work and time.

Teach one phase of the break at a time. The best way of installing the fast break is to introduce certain phases of it one at a time. At first it is best to try to teach the breaking patterns of the three lane break. More than likely it will take all year to master these patterns well. However, you should not become discouraged if at times the players fail to use the patterns well. The defenses set up may hamper the break so that it becomes ineffectual. As you learn more and more about the break, you will be able to adjust your offense to the defense as pointed out above. If the break sputters at times, the weakness is not in the break itself but in the teaching of it.

Teach the break from different zones. You should not wait until the team has completely mastered one phase of it before introducing another phase. When you are relatively certain that your players have understood and mastered one phase of the break, even though at times their execution is amateurish, you can introduce another phase. It is best to teach the break from various zones because you will find it sound to change defenses to keep the opponents baffled. If you teach the 2–1–2 zone break, you can next introduce it from the 3–2, followed by a 2–3 or 1–3–1. Once the players have learned to break into a three lane pattern, they will experience little difficulty in adjusting to the other zone breaks. Here, again, caution must be exercised. If you encounter difficulty in teaching new phases, it is better not to rush your teaching. Give the boys more time before attempting it again.

It is better to underteach than to overteach. More than likely it will take all season to teach the boys to break from the several zones. The first year it is better to underteach than to overteach. You may well be satisfied if you are able to teach successfully the three lane breaks from the several zones. How well your team masters these patterns depends on your personnel. It is conceivable, though not likely, that you may have players who can assimilate all phases of the fast break in one year. If you are blessed with such personnel, by all means teach all phases.

Knowledge of basketball fundamentals is necessary before break is taught. You will find that your players will master the fast break fundamentals more readily if they have adequately mastered the fundamentals of dribbling, passing, and shooting. If they have not, they will experience difficulty in executing plays rapidly which they cannot execute slowly. In such a case, you will probably be better off to delay teaching the fast break until the boys have mastered the fundamentals of basketball.

Much is learned during the first year. From the caution expressed above the reader may get the impression that the first year is a total loss. The writer does not wish to convey this impression at all. He merely wishes the reader to know that he should not expect too much the first year. Nevertheless, the first year should bring results. Undoubtedly, the team will improve upon the record of the previous year. The greatest success of this first year is a hidden one—the planting of fast break principles in the players' minds. The results will be seen immediately on the first day of practice of the second year. The boys will break automatically the moment they are on the offense. They will handle the ball better on passes and on shots. They will dribble better into offensive territory. They will visualize fast break opportunities better. Instinctively they will break when opportunities are present and will slow down at other times, while during the first year they break at all times, often trying to force their way through a set defense.

Introduce fire-horse patterns the second year. During the second year you can introduce the patterns from out-of-bounds. Since the break from this position requires split second timing, it is better to wait until the second year before attempting to install it into the offense. Once the boys have mastered breaking from rebounds, they will be ready for fire-horse basketball. Although you may content yourself with the more controlled break from rebounding, you may wish to teach the fire-horse type to keep in reserve for use at several points in the game. When the defense is accustomed to having the offense bring the ball down court slowly after a score, it may tend to lag. At such times the alert team may use fire-horse patterns to catch the defense off guard.

This offense is necessary for certain teams. You may wish to reserve this special offense for certain teams. If your opponents have unusually tall men, so that breaking from rebounds may be difficult, it may be necessary to use this race type of offense. If your players lack the height to break successfully from rebounds, you may decide to use a press defense in order to break from it.

Introduce other phases of fast breaking. The second year will be a good time to introduce the other phases of the fast break. Teach players how to break after a missed foul, since many such opportunities will arise during the game. Teach them how to break after a center tap and after a held ball.

Slow down attack when the defense is set. In order to teach when to break and when not to, you can instruct the back court men to yell, "Slow." This will advise the players that it is wiser to use deliberate patterns than to force their way through a set defense. You may find it more practical to have any player, who notices a set defense, yell this precaution.

Have a long-range program in mind. During the first year you may find blending the fast break with a deliberate pattern quite a task, requiring all your skill in teaching. You may be forced to explain again and again when to break and when to slow down. Above all you must never be discouraged with temporary failures. Keep a long range program in mind, knowing that the fast break will bring you results which you could not achieve otherwise. Hide your disappointments from your players, who are sensitive to such feelings in their coach.

THE EXPERIENCED COACH

The experienced coach who moves to a new school situation is confronted with a different type of psychological problem. He must convince the boys that the system he wishes to introduce is superior. Therein lies his problem. If you, as an experienced coach, wish to install a fast break system, you will have to sell them on the superiority of the break. Your task will be even greater if your predecessor used a different system and was successful with it. However, by giving a brief history of fast break basketball and its success everywhere, you may influence your players to learn it.

If you had exceptional success with the style elsewhere, you should modestly present this fact in order to gain the confidence of your players. This confidence in you is more necessary if your predecessor was very successful.

Too many coaches disregard the feelings of their players, little realizing that their success depends on the emotional attitude of their players. A coach who can keep his players confident will win more games than one who knows more but cannot sell his knowledge to his players.

Undo slow break habits. Before you can teach fast break basketball, you must undo slow break habits. A player who is accustomed to a more deliberate style will experience great difficulty at first when he attempts to quick break. That is where you must exercise psychology on your players and on yourself also. You must prepare the boys for the expected difficulties, explaining to them that it is extremely hard to change from one style of attack to another without experiencing problems. By promising them patient treatment, you will encourage your boys to make a harmonious transition in offense. Today this problem is not as trying as it was ten years ago, since most basketball players have been sold on the superiority of the fast break.

Personnel will determine success. It goes without saying that a coach who attempts to teach the quick break to a group of boys who have not used it before can expect more trouble than the coach who teaches it to a group which is accustomed to it. Depending on your personnel, you may expect this first year to be an experimental one. It will take time before you know your personnel well. Until you do, you cannot determine which players can best fit into your style. The progress you make is also dependent on the assimilating powers of your players as well as on their adjustability.

Defeatist attitude must be overcome before success comes.
The problem of the coach attempting to introduce the fast break
to a school in the throes of defeats is even more trying. He not only
must teach a different style of ball but must also instill confidence
in his players. Since a team that has lost consistently has developed
a defeatist attitude, you can expect games lost through this mental
attitude. Your players will miss chance after chance on layups. Because the success of Fast Break basketball is predicated on the ability
of the players to make layup shots, games will be lost that should be
won easily. Ranting and criticizing will not help. The coach must
constantly show the players how successful they would be if they
had more confidence in their ability.

By explaining that these easy layups are the key to success, he
will eventually help the boys develop confidence. Nevertheless, it
takes success to develop confidence, and one unexpected victory will
do more to establish confidence than a thousand words from you.
Therefore, you can only continue to encourage your players while
waiting for this unexpected victory.

DAILY PRACTICE SCHEDULE

THE DAILY PRACTICE SCHEDULE REMAINS FAIRLY UNIFORM, EXCEPT for changes which unexpected situations bring about. The fast break patterns are practiced every day, since only through daily practice can we hope to make breaking automatic. Scrimmage takes place every day because it maintains top physical condition and helps keep breaking at a peak.

MONDAY

3:00—3:15	Run 20 laps around the gym.
3:15—3:45	Practice layup shots from right, left, and center areas.
3:45—4:00	Practice set shots from all angles. Fouls are taken on basket at other end of floor.
4:00—4:15	Discuss mistakes of Friday's game.
4:15—4:45	Practice fast break patterns.
4:45—5:30	Scrimmage.

TUESDAY

3:00—3:15	Run laps around gym. Skip rope.
3:15—3:45	Practice layup shots.
3:45—4:00	Practice set shots and fouls.
4:00—4:15	Practice rebounding.
4:15—4:45	Practice fast break patterns.
4:45—5:15	Practice against opponent's patterns.
5:15—5:45	Scrimmage.

WEDNESDAY

3:00—3:15	Run laps.
3:15—3:30	Layup shots.
3:30—3:45	Set shots and fouls.
3:45—4:15	Fast break patterns.

4:15—4:45	Practice out-of-bounds plays.
	Practice held balls. Practice tap-offs.
4:45—5:00	Practice against opponent plays.
5:00—5:45	Scrimmage.

THURSDAY

3:00—3:15	Run laps. Skip rope for agility.
3:15—3:40	Layup shots.
3:40—4:00	Set shots and fouls.
4:00—4:20	Fast break patterns.
4:20—4:40	Practice against press defense.
4:40—4:50	Practice rebounding.
4:50—5:10	Practice defense. Practice against opponent plays.
5:10—5:40	Scrimmage.

FRIDAY

| 3:00—3:30 | Practice set shots. Practice foul shots. Practice layup shots. |

There are several items in the daily schedule which need explaining. As the reader can readily notice, much time is spent on shooting. Since the success of fast break basketball is so dependent on shooting, too much stress cannot be placed on this phase of the game.

The daily practice session appears too long. However, long periods are required to maintain peak physical condition. Some coaches may fear staleness. The writer has found that too much time cannot be given to practice. As long as the boys are relaxed during the practice period, they will not suffer from too much practice.

The Friday practice seems superfluous. Boys will fret the afternoon of the game, using up much valuable nervous energy. The half hour practice will be better for the boys as they will be together and the tension is off. In addition, the practice of shooting makes it easier for them at night. They will be sharper in their shooting.

The daily schedule suggested above need not be binding. It should be flexible. If you find that one phase needs more attention, then deviate from the schedule. You may find it necessary to stress certain phases and minimize others. A good coach uses his own judgment.

As the season progresses, the daily schedule varies because the coach will wish to introduce new fundamentals or strategies. The following changes may serve as a guide:

MONDAY

3:00—3:30   Layup and set shots.
3:30—4:00   3–2 zone defense.
4:00—4:30   Closing minutes strategy.
4:30—5:00   Press defense for Fast Breaking.
5:00—5:30   Scrimmage.

TUESDAY

3:00—3:30   Layup and set shots.
3:30—4:00   2–1–2 zone defense.
4:00—4:30   Last minute strategy.
4:30—5:00   Fast Breaking after a foul.
5:00—5:30   Scrimmage.

WEDNESDAY

3:00—3:30   Layup and set shots.
3:30—4:00   2–3 zone defense.
4:00—4:30   Offense against the press.
4:30—5:00   Fast Breaking after a held ball.
5:00—5:30   Scrimmage.

THURSDAY

3:00—3:30   Layup and set shots.
3:30—4:00   1–3–1 zone defense.
4:00—4:30   Fire-horse basketball.
4:30—5:00   Multiple defense.
5:00—5:30   Scrimmage.

Select whichever fundamentals you wish to practice. You may not desire to practice all types of zones, selecting only one or two for use. You may decide not to use fire-horse basketball. However, whichever fundamentals you feel should be incorporated into your fast break system can be inserted into your regular schedule.

Another point to remember as the season progresses is not to stop practicing the fundamentals of the early season schedule. Return to them for review at least once a week. A schedule, at best, is a guide and should be elastic. If the boys do not grasp a fundamental, deviate from your proposed schedule and devote the time necessary to teach them the skills needed. Games will also determine which part of the schedule to follow. Common sense is important in setting up a routine.

INDEX

A

Anderson, Winston, 87
Area of break, in scouting speed, 155
Arizin, Paul, 2
Assignments, during time outs, 140
Attacks, slowing down, 160

B

Back court press, and stolen passes, 143
Ball retention, when ahead, 140
Barnstable High School, 141
Barnstable vs Bourne, 141
Baseball pass, 3, 55
Basketball drills, in pre-season training, 10-11
Bergen County tournaments, 157
Boredom with drills, tactics to overcome, 12-13
Boston Celtics, 2, 6, 112
Boston Garden, 1949 state tournament at, 141
Bottle (1-2-2) zone defense, 4
Bounce passes, 3
Bourne vs Barnstable, 141
Breaking:
  against press defense, 86-87
  from a man-to-man defense, 85
  from 1-3-1 zone, 85
  from press defense, 86
  from a 3-2 zone, 72
  from a 2-1-2 zone, 56-58, 71
  from a 2-3 zone, 71-72

C

Calisthenics for leg development, 9

Calverly, Ernest, 55
Canastota High School:
  vs Camden, 130
  vs Hamilton, 87
  vs Richfield, 87
  vs Vernon-Verona-Sherril (V.V.S.), 129-130
Cape Cod league games, 141
Cape May vs Glassboro, 86-87
C.C.N.Y. (College of the City of New York), 55
Center tap, break after, 160
Centers:
  rebounding skill of, 8
  selection of, 7
  in 2-1-2 zone, 56-58, 71
  in 2-3 zone, 71
Chances, when ahead, 140
Chest passes, 3
Cliffside Park High School, 54
Closing minutes, strategy for, 140-141
Coaches:
  Keaney, Frank, 53
  Lapchick, Joe, 142
  problems of, 161-162
  Russell, Bill, 6, 112
  strategy, 131-132, 138-141
Combination man-to-man zone defense, 129-130
Confidence, establishment of, 161-162
Connecticut vs Dartmouth, 139
Controlled fast break, 40
Co-ordination in shooting, 1-2
Corner shooting, against 1-3-1 zone defense, 156-157
Corner shooting, in 3-2 zone defense, 114, 156
Corpus Christi High School, 87

167

Court strategy, 131-132, 138-141
Cousy, Bob, 2
Cross country running, 10

D

Dartmouth vs Connecticut, 139
Defeatist attitudes, 162
Defenses:
 against fast break teams, 142-143,
  151-153
 changes during games, 139
 clogging middle lane, 151
 deliberate attacks to slow down
  breaks, 152-153
 for fast break teams, 112-115, 128-130
 man-to-man *see* Man-to-man defense
 multiple, 128-130
 press *see* Press defenses
 scouting, 156-157
 strategy against fast break teams,
  142-143, 151-153
 switches during time outs, 139
 two men back, 143, 151
 zone, 3-4, 113-115 *see also* Zone
  defenses
Defensive skill of forwards, 5-6
Deliberate attacks, to slow down breaks,
 152-153
Deliberate plays, 88, 110-111
Double pivot plays, 110-111
Dribbling, 2, 13-14, 40
Drills:
 basketball, 10-11
 boredom with, 12-13
 for centers, 58
 dribbling, 2, 13-14
 for fast break, 4
 four-on-three fast break, 27
 layup shots, 12-13
 pass outs, 13
 pre-season training, 9-11
 reaction time, 7
 rebounding, 8, 13
 shooting, 1-2, 14
 three-on-two fast breaks, 26-27
 two-on-one fast breaks, 14, 26

E

Emotional attitudes of players, 161
Encouragement, in time outs, 139

F

Fire-horse basketball, 41, 53-55, 157,
 160
Fire-horse teams, 142-143
First year, teaching of, 159-160
Forwards:
 selection of, 5-6
 in 2-1-2 zone defense, 56, 57, 58, 71,
  113
 in 2-3 zone defense, 71, 114
Fouls, opportunities after, 28, 160
Four-on-three fast break, 27
Fundamentals:
 dribbling, 13-14
 four-on-three fast break, 27
 knowledge of, 159
 layup shots, 12-13
 pass outs, 13
 practice of, 164, 165
 shooting, 14
 three-on-two fast breaks, 26-27
 two-on-one fast break, 14, 26

G

Georgia Military College, 111
Glassboro vs Cape May, 86-87
Guards:
 rebounding skill of, 8, 13
 selection of, 6
 in three-on-two fast break, 26
 in 2-1-2 zone, 56, 57, 58, 71
 in 2-3 zone, 71-72

H

Hackensack vs North Arlington, 157
Hamilton vs Canastota, 87
Height, of forwards, 5
Held balls, opportunities after, 38, 160
Held balls, when ahead, 140
Hook passes, 3
Hot teams, time outs for, 139

K

Keaney, Frank, 53

L

Lapchick, Joe, 142